FINISHING A HOUSE

FINISHING A HOUSE

A COMPLETE GUIDE
from Installing Insulation to Running Trim

ROE OSBORN

The Taunton Press

The Taunton Press, Inc., 63 South Main Street, PO Box 5506, Newtown, CT 06470-5506
e-mail: tp@taunton.com

Editors: Alex Giannini, Peter Chapman

Copy editor: Seth Reichgott

Indexer: Jay Kreider

Cover design: Scott Santoro, Worksight

Interior design and layout: Scott Santoro, Worksight

Layout coordinator: Amy Griffin

Illustrators: Christopher Mills, except for the illustration on p. 5: drawing by Don Mannes, *Fine Homebuilding,* © by The Taunton Press, Inc.

Photographers: Roe Osborn, except for photos on p. 53 (top right): Justin Fink, *Fine Homebuilding,* © by The Taunton Press, Inc., p. 53 (bottom): *Fine Homebuilding,* © by The Taunton Press, Inc., p. 212 (bottom): *Fine Homebuilding,* © by The Taunton Press, Inc., p. 213 (all photos): *Fine Homebuilding,* © by The Taunton Press, Inc.

The following names/manufacturers appearing in *Finishing a House* are trademarks:
Flex Tape®, Styrofoam®

Library of Congress Cataloging-in-Publication Data

Osborn, Roe.

  Finishing a house : a complete guide from installing insulation to running trim / Roe Osborn.

       pages cm

   ISBN 978-1-60085-393-7 (pbk.)

1. Carpentry. 2. House construction. I. Title.

  TH5606.O83 2012

  698--dc23

                                    2011050357

Printed in the United States of America

10 9 8 7 6 5 4 3 2 1

To my parents, George and Gab Osborn, who unfailingly and unconditionally supported me in all the diverse paths my life has taken.

ACKNOWLEDGMENTS

I owe an amazing debt of thanks to the many people who have shared their knowledge and skills with me over the years, so at least I sound like I know what I am talking about. Again thanks to Rob Turnquist—who sent me to that closet to run baseboard—but who always shared his craftsmanship and knowledge freely. Thanks also to the amazing craftsmen I got to work with at the boat shop, where my finish carpentry skills increased exponentially in a short time. Thanks as well to all the incredible carpenters I met and worked with while at *Fine Homebuilding* magazine.

Working with the people on the projects that I used for this book reinforced all the feelings I have about the incredible generosity of craftspeople in their willingness to share their knowledge. Each of them at every level enthusiastically answered all of my questions and never griped about me stopping them for that extra photo. There were dozens of individuals who helped me, but here is a list of the companies that those folks worked for. Thanks to Peter Donovan of Donovan Building Corp., as well as to Gable Building Corp., who allowed me to use their projects for my photos. Thanks to Gable project manager, April Ducott, for keeping me on the project schedule. Thanks to Cape Associates Builders, Cape Cod Insulation, Barber Drywall, Krikorian Hardwood Floors, Billy McGraw of William McGraw Carpentry, Dennis Buchelt of DWB Custom Interior Trim, Classic Kitchens and Interiors, Kimberly Gilmore Tile Design, and Angelo Aquino Painting.

On the personal side, thanks to Humphrey, my sole surviving Jack Russell terrier, who always accompanied me enthusiastically on the many trips to the job sites in the back of my car. Thanks also to my growing network of friends out here on Cape Cod who continue to support and push me in my endeavors. And finally an extra special thanks to my best friend and partner, Laurie Sullivan, who had infinite patience through this whole process, and who has managed to rekindle my self confidence and hope while letting me rediscover the joy of being part of a true team.

CONTENTS

INTRODUCTION

When I wrote my first book, *Framing a House*, I used to tell everyone that it was like house framing for dummies—and that they'd chosen the right guy to write it! I was amazed when professional framers had positive things to say about the book. I soon realized that the information hadn't been dumbed down at all; it was just presented in understandable language and in a highly visual format. This book is written in that same spirit.

If you're reading this book as a guide or reference for finishing a home (or even just a room) that you plan to build yourself, chances are that you have some experience with finish work, and that you have some idea of the process. This book is not a step-by-step guide as much as it is an "approach" guide. You may choose different materials or different looks in your finished project, but this book should give you the basics for getting started regardless. One thing I would suggest for your personal reference as well as for archival purposes is to take lots of pictures. Photograph every room at every stage, especially the bare framing and roughed-in systems. Then create a scrapbook. You'll find that the scrapbook isn't just something nice to brag about with your friends, but it will come in handy 10 or more years down the road when you might want to take a wall out or add a door. A quick glance at your scrapbook can save countless headaches when you know what's behind that drywall.

If this book is a reference for a career that you've just begun, please realize that despite its simplicity, this book was born of countless hours both as a contractor and as an editor. I approached each chapter the way I approached articles when I was an editor at *Fine Homebuilding*: I asked a million questions and took pictures of every tiny step, no matter how seemingly insignificant. Quite often I discovered that the mastery and the craftsmanship were in those microsteps. A friend with whom I worked in the joiner shop at the boatyard used to call these shortcuts that make the job more professional. If you're embarking on a career in homebuilding, be a sponge with your eyes, ears, and hands. Watch the experienced members of the crew and never hesitate to ask questions. Listen to the answers and then try the methods yourself. The best craftsmen accumulate knowledge and skills until the day they finally hang up their tool belts.

No matter what background you come from, I offer these words of caution before you begin:

- Always think through a process before jumping in.
- If there's something you don't understand, find a craftsman who will take the time to explain a process or a procedure. There are many skilled builders who are willing to share their knowledge with people willing to learn.
- If a process doesn't seem safe to you, then it probably isn't. Find a way to do every task safely.
- Always do your prep work before performing a task. That may mean building safe scaffolding, or setting up a work table, or re-routing hoses and extension cords. Whatever the task, proper preparation will make the job go more smoothly and more safely.
- Wear safety equipment! Professionals are notorious for *not* using proper protection—sometimes out of ignorance and sometimes from a false sense of pride.

Good luck, have fun, and build safe!

Roe Osborn

Before You Tackle the Interior

The last roof shingle is on and the last clapboard is nailed in place. Your house is officially "weathered in," as they say in the building trades. Time to jump on the interior, right? Not so fast, Mr. Eager Beaver! Just as with the house framing, there is a proper sequence to finishing the inside of your house. And before you start insulating and hanging drywall, you have to make sure that your house is completely ready for those steps in the process. Let's take a look at all the things that should be completed before you can begin your work.

Double-Check the Rough Electric

In every part of this country I've worked or visited, a house cannot be built without an electrical plan. But the electrical plan is just that: a plan. Code requires outlets every certain number of feet on each wall, and the same goes for above a kitchen countertop. When the plan is drawn up, it's usually to satisfy those requirements. What the plan might not know is that you have a brigade of small appliances, many of which might need to be plugged in at the same time. Those two receptacles over the countertop just won't cut it. It also might not know that you're going to be putting your bed against that south wall, and that you and your partner would like separate reading lights on either side of the bed. In other words the rough electric should be installed to satisfy your individual needs as well as the code requirements.

Typical Electric Plan

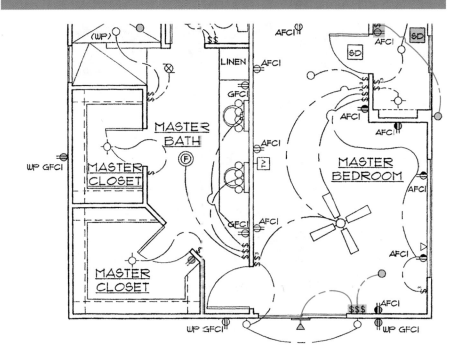

Although code requires a certain minimal distance between receptacles on walls (top) and above kitchen counters (above), make sure you have enough for your needs and in the specific places you'll need them.

Learn Your Electrician's Shorthand

When checking the rough electrical work, you'll find a lot of writing on the edges of the framing akin to hieroglyphics. This writing is the electrician's shorthand to identify and locate every electrical box and circuit in the house. Electrical symbols are not universal, so it pays to familiarize yourself with your electrician's labels. Knowing the labels makes it easy to figure out what each electrical box is for and lets you understand the electrician's strategy. Also, many wires are left in walls without boxes. Each of those should be labeled as well (see the photo below).

Electrician's Labels

Electricians go through a house after rough framing and label the locations of different wiring elements. Here are some examples:

 Duplex receptacle

 Ground Fault receptacle
GFCI

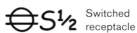**S½** Switched receptacle

S SW Single-pole switch

S₃ Three-way switch

S₄ Four-way switch

TSTAT Thermostat

Check the labels on any wire that is left in a wall without an electrical box.

Receptacles

Go through every room and visualize where your furniture will be placed. If it's a living room or den, determine where the couch and other seating will go. It might make sense to draw a sketch showing the sizes of your furniture and exactly where you see everything going. Along with the seating comes lighting. Make sure there is a nearby receptacle for table lamps and floor lamps for reading as well as for general illumination. One area to pay special attention to is the entertainment center location. You should know where the TV and stereo are going to be installed. You should also have an idea of how many different electrical devices you'll need receptacles for. Those might include a TV, receiver, DVD player, CD changer, and turntable. Don't depend on plug strips and extension cords to supply power for all these items. It might be a good idea for the electrician to run a dedicated circuit for all the electronic devices. Your electrician also needs to know every kitchen appliance that is being permanently installed. Dishwashers, garbage disposals, built-in microwave ovens, as well as regular electric ovens and stovetops, all require electricity, and the proper power supplies need to be provided for each.

Adding a circuit for lighting or for receptacles is fairly easy before the interior finish goes on. It becomes a complicated mess afterward. Any electrician worth his or her salt should have gone over every detail of the plan with you to make sure it serves your needs.

Entertainment system goes here. Make sure there will be plenty of electricity for all the components. If there are lots of them, a dedicated circuit might not be a bad idea.

Make sure there is electricity supplied to all the permanent kitchen appliances. In this photo, the box below is for the dishwasher and the label for the garbage disposal is above.

Switched receptacles are a good idea for rooms without general lighting. Put the switch near the entry to the room and make sure the receptacle is near a lamp position.

So, what do you get when you cross a switch with a receptacle? That's right—a switched receptacle or a switched plug. This situation usually involves having half of a duplex receptacle (two plugs) controlled by a standard wall switch. A switched receptacle is handy when you want to turn on a light when you enter a room without general lighting, such as ceiling cans or sconces. A lamp plugged into the switched receptacle is left in the "on" position so the wall switch controls it. A good way to test the necessity for switched receptacles is to go through your rough-framed house in the dark. As you walk into a room, imagine yourself reaching for a switch or walking over to a lamp. If that walk involves groping about in the dark, it might be wise to have the electrician install a switched receptacle. Again, at this stage, adding the extra box with the switch wire is pretty simple. Later on? Not so much.

Overhead lighting is important not only for illuminating a room but also for spotlighting wall hangings. Make sure you've planned for both.

Lighting

If you plan to display art on the walls of your living room (or any other room for that matter), consider small overhead spotlights or a track light if there is more than one or two spots to illuminate. Along with the fixtures, determine a logical and convenient place for a switch to control the lights. Again, the electrician can add these items a lot more easily and inexpensively at this juncture than after the drywall is installed.

We already discussed receptacle needs in the kitchen. But perhaps more important is the kitchen lighting. Imagine yourself, apron on, preparing a complex meal. You may have three or more work areas for prepping and cooking food. Each of these areas should have adequate light, and most often that light will be overhead. Pay particular attention to the sink area and any kitchen island or kitchen soffits. Again, if you've overlooked any of these areas, remedy the situation before the drywall goes on.

Dimmer Switches

It's not too early to think about the switches that will control lights such as ceiling cans and sconces. I can't tell you how many high-end houses I've had to photograph where the lights were controlled by simple on-off switches instead of dimmer switches. An absence of dimmers is a sure sign of a builder spec house, where every extra cost, such as dimmers, is eliminated. In these houses, if you want to lower the lights you need to change the lightbulbs. Dimmer switches cost a bit more than regular on-off switches, but compared to the convenience they provide, the cost of dimmers is minimal. And using dimmers can prolong the life of your lightbulbs while using less electricity. Let your electrician know which circuits you want controlled by dimmers, as it might affect the wiring strategy.

Pay special attention to the lighting locations in the kitchen. Each task area should have its own overhead lighting, such as over the sink.

Bathrooms are usually pretty well planned out ahead of time. You should know where the bathing area will be along with the toilet and vanity or bathroom sink. Each of these areas needs proper lighting—especially the bathroom sink, where you prepare yourself for the day. Each set of lights should be controlled by its own switch for maximum efficiency. And don't forget exhaust fans in the bathrooms with showers or baths. Ideally these fixtures should be installed and ducted at the time of the rough inspection. Combination fan/light units can be a great way to provide general illumination in a bathroom. If you do install fan/light combination units, have the electrician install separate switches for the fan and the light.

Switches and Doors

As you go through each room, be aware of which way the door to the room will swing. Make sure that the door in the open position does not block the switches. In most cases the choice of switch position versus door swing is obvious, but other times it can be more subtle, such as when the door swing has been reversed to accommodate furniture or some other obstacle.

In the bathroom, separate switches should control the lights for the toilet, the shower, and the vanity.

Communications wiring

This area is probably the most challenging of all to deal with. You probably know where your office or home computer station will be. But what about the kids' computers or setting up a computer in the kitchen? In this "wireless" age, the computer dilemma might have an easy solution, but you still have to determine the best place to locate the wireless router and make sure

Make sure that exhaust fans are installed and properly ducted before the rough inspection.

Communications wires should go to a hub that's in a logical place. A board mounted on the basement wall will hold the terminal.

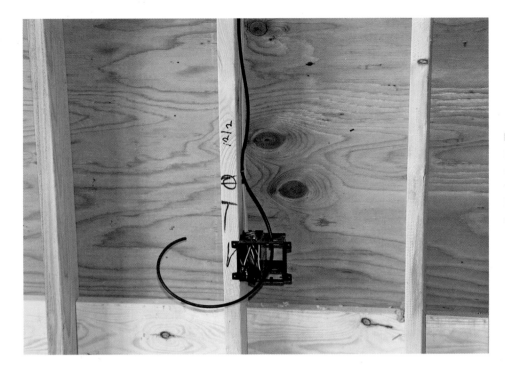

Nearly every room in a new house is equipped for cable TV. These boxes house both the receptacle and the cable wire.

the proper input wire is in place at that location (see the bottom right photo on p. 9).

The next item is the phone network. I recall my brother building an addition and wanting a telephone in every room—including the bathroom. I thought he was crazy at the time. Now I might be more willing to consider that option. At the very least you should make sure that there is a telephone jack conveniently located in every major room: living room, den, bedrooms (especially the master bedroom), kitchen, and the bathrooms if you just can't live without that amenity. In this day and age, old-style telephone wire is rarely used. Newer CATV wire gives you more options, including the option to interlink your computers and your phones. If you have a complex system, make sure your electrician is experienced and qualified to install this type of wiring. And don't forget the most important communications wire to most people: the cable TV connection. Most new homes and additions have cable hook-ups in every room but the closets (photo above). Finally, if your house is to have an electronic security system, those wires need to be in place as well.

Check Rough Plumbing

Plumbing is a little more cast in stone (or usually copper) than the rough wiring. The plumber roughs in stubs or hot and cold piping to supply every sink, as well as every bathtub and shower. There should also be a cold-water supply for every toilet. Make sure you haven't forgotten the laundry area. Most plumbers install a laundry "station" that houses the supply as well as the drain in a convenient unit that mounts in between wall studs. Make sure the dryer vent is in place as well at this stage.

Exit plumbing is also crucial, but at this point your plumber has already ordered the toilets and has hopefully set the closet flange (toilet drain) out the right distance from the wall to accommodate those toilets. The inspector should check to make sure that every exit line is properly vented, and that cleanouts have been installed where needed. Again, any changes to the system should happen now before insulation and drywall go in.

Be sure that your plumber has run hot and cold water supplies to every sink (below) and to every tub or shower (bottom left). Those supplies should be pressure tested as well. Laundry areas have a special hookup system (bottom right). Be sure the dryer exhaust vent is also in place.

Toilets are sized by the distance the closet flange is from the wall. Double-check to ensure the toilets you chose will fit properly, and that each toilet has a cold-water supply.

Cleanouts are an essential part of the exit plumbing.

Piping Options

The pipes used in plumbing continue to evolve. My folks' house from the 1950s had copper supply pipes and then copper drains that were soldered into larger cast-iron pipes for the exit plumbing. In the 1960s and 1970s, PVC (polyvinyl chloride) replaced the copper and cast-iron exit plumbing. But PVC pipe is noisy. Water rushing down the pipe seems to be amplified. So there is a move back to cast-iron piping where waste lines pass through noise-sensitive spaces such as a living room. At the ceiling the PVC pipe is tied into cast iron with sleeves and clamps. Then at the floor the cast iron ties back into the PVC before it heads to the sewer or septic system (see the photo at right). This system takes advantage of each material's strong points: the workability and flexibility of the PVC and the quiet of the cast iron.

Copper is still the supply material of choice, but in the last few decades a new product known as PEX tubing (cross-linked polyethylene) has been making inroads. At first there were many problems with PEX tubing, mostly having to do with the fittings that joined the pipe together. But now the fittings have improved dramatically and plumbers seem to have adopted a hybrid between PEX tubing and copper tubing for supply lines. Copper is used where the water enters the house, but then runs of PEX pipe feed the various areas of the house. PEX comes in long lengths and is flexible enough to be fed through joists without having to install labor-intensive fittings. The PEX joins back with copper piping at the fixture to allow standard fittings to be attached for installation (see the photo below).

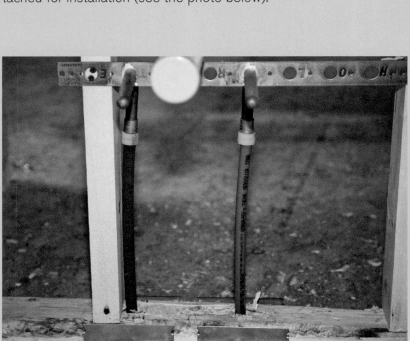

Where second-floor plumbing passes through first-floor walls, PVC pipe joins cast-iron pipe to keep the plumbing noise to a minimum (above). PEX plastic pipe is quicker and more efficient to run in the framing than copper, but copper is needed to attach the fixture fittings (left).

One area that's often overlooked is the water supply for kitchen appliances. The dishwasher is obvious, but if you've planned for an ice maker or for fresh water and ice from your refrigerator, make sure the plumber is aware of any extra supply lines that might need to get piped in.

Check also for cold-water supplies for outdoor water faucets, also called hose bibbs or sill cocks. Adding one of these is usually not a big deal after the insulation is installed, but most plumbers prefer to run all their supply lines before the insulation goes in.

Another task for the plumber is the piping for natural gas or propane-powered appliances. These can include the stove or range, clothes dryer, water heater, and furnace or boiler. Again, make sure that the plumber is aware of all the gas/propane appliances you plan to install.

Hose bibbs should be installed before the rough inspection. Check to make sure you have a convenient number of them around the perimeter of your house.

Double-Check All Framing Details

Before you call for the rough inspection, go over every square inch of the interior framing. First check every corner to make sure there is ample nailing on both sides for drywall. Remember that drywall on an adjacent wall takes up at least ½ in. of space on the nailer. If the nailer was cheated into place with only 1 in. exposed, that means there's only ½ in. left to catch the edge of the drywall. If you find this situation, add scrap 2× to give the drywallers plenty to nail or screw into. Furring strips usually take care of the ceilings, but make sure the edges of the ceiling have been detailed to catch the drywall properly.

Also look for other places where nailers might come in handy. Measure up the height of the kitchen cabinets and put in 2× blocking for attaching the top back edge of the cabinets. Also add nailers for handrail support along a stair wall. When you go to install the handrail later on, you'll thank yourself. Another place that I always forget to add backing is for towel-bar support in the bathrooms. Again, picture yourself getting out of the shower or bath and reaching for a towel. A solid 2× nailer in the wall will ensure that the towel holders can be installed where they are most convenient. And most important of all, put in blocking for the toilet paper holder.

Finally, make sure that metal plates have been installed on the framing to protect plumbing or electrical lines in the wall. You may think these things are a pain, but an errant nail or screw can cause a leak, and tearing out a wall to fix it is exponentially more aggravating.

Check each corner for nailers to attach drywall. Add extra 2× nailers if need be.

Blocking should be added in anticipation of items that need solid attachment. For example, blocks at the height of the kitchen cabinets streamline their installation.

Blocking for handrails

Blocking for finish material

Blocking can take the guesswork out of attaching finish material as well as handrails along stairs.

Blocks can mean that your towel rack is in the most convenient spot (top). Don't forget blocking for the all-important toilet paper holder (above).

Don't skimp on the metal protective plates. These babies can save costly plumbing leaks from wayward nails or screws.

Insulating Your House

If you think of the house framing as a skeleton and the exterior finish as skin, then the insulation could be described as a layer of fat. Just as fat helps keep our body temperature warm and stable, insulation is a key part of making the house inhabitable. Insulation also helps a house perform efficiently, keeping the inside comfortable in the extreme heat of summer as well as the cold of winter. Insulation does not provide the warmth inside the house, but like fat, it keeps that warmth from escaping through the outer shell.

In most houses, insulation is the last thing to go into the wall cavities before the interior finish materials go on. For the past few decades, fiberglass has been the insulation of choice. But with all the recent focus on energy efficiency, many different kinds of insulation have been developed that perform differently in different situations. Most new types of insulation require specialized tools and skills for installation, so this chapter deals with installing fiberglass, which is still the most common option.

How Does Insulation Work?

The key word here is *comfort*. We all want to keep the inside of our homes comfortable: warm in the winter, cool in the summer. Any heat that our house gives up in the winter has to be replaced by our heating system to keep us comfortable. Likewise, any heat gained inside the house from the summer sun needs to be removed by air movement or an air conditioner. Insulation in ceilings, floors, and walls slows down or resists the movement of heat through those surfaces.

Insulation and moisture

Warm air can hold more moisture than cold air, and as air moves naturally from warm to cold, it gives up moisture that condenses on cold surfaces, such as the back side of wall sheathing. Excess moisture can be absorbed by the insulation, making it less effective. To prevent moisture from moving into the wall cavity and condensing there, a vapor barrier must be used on the inside surfaces of walls as well as the uppermost ceilings in a house. Fiberglass insulation is available with a vapor barrier attached. That barrier is designed to prevent moisture from passing into the wall cavity. As a rule, the vapor barrier should always be installed facing the living space of a building. In ceilings it should be installed facing down.

Holes drilled in wall plates are penetrations in the building envelope and create paths for warm air to escape. Seal around holes for electric wires (top) or plumbing vents (above), with expanding foam that is sprayed into the holes.

Before the Insulation Goes In

One of the catch phrases in creating energy-efficient homes is "sealing the envelope." This phrase refers to making the outer shell of a house tight to keep the conditioned air (heated or cooled) inside where it belongs. The building envelope of a home consists of the foundation, the first floor, the exterior walls, and the attic or roof, depending on the design. Any breach or uninsulated part of this envelope is a path for conditioned air to escape.

R-values

Our society did not really become energy conscious until the energy crisis of the 1970s. Suddenly, putting insulation into homes became much more critical. Soon after, the Department of Energy (DOE) created a standard to measure the effectiveness of insulation. That standard is called the R-value, or an insulation's ability to resist heat transfer. The greater the number, the better the insulation is at keeping heat where it belongs. Each type of insulation is assigned an R-value. For example, the R-value of fiberglass is 3.17 per in. The R-value your house needs depends a lot on the climate you live in. The DOE developed a system of zones throughout the country along with a chart that lists the recommended amount of insulation for each zone.

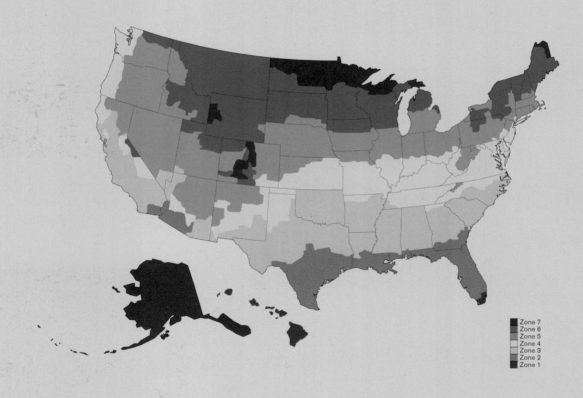

■ Zone 7
■ Zone 6
■ Zone 5
□ Zone 4
■ Zone 3
■ Zone 2
■ Zone 1

(A) R-18, R-22, and R-28 exterior wall systems can be achieved by either cavity insulation or cavity insulation with insulating sheathing. For 2×4 walls, use either 3½-in.-thick R-15 or 3½-in.-thick R-13 fiberglass insulation with insulating sheathing. For 2×6 walls, use either 5½-in.-thick R-21 or 6¼-in.-thick R-19 fiberglass insulation.

(B) Insulate crawlspace walls only if the crawlspace is dry all year, the floor above is not insulated, and all ventilation to the craw space is blocked. A vapor retarder (e.g., 4-mil or 6-mil polyethylene film) should be installed on the ground to reduce moisture migration into the crawlspace.

(C) No slab edge insulation is recommended.

Zone	Gas	Heat Pump	Fuel Oil	Ceiling Attic	Ceiling Cathedral	Wall (A)	Floor	Crawlspace (B)	Slab Edge	Basement Interior	Basement Exterior
1	x	x	x	R-49	R-38	R-18	R-25	R-19	R-8	R-11	R-10
2	x	x	x	R-49	R-38	R-18	R-25	R-19	R-8	R-11	R-10
3	x	x	x	R-49	R-38	R-18	R-25	R-19	R-8	R-11	R-10
4	x	x	x	R-38	R-38	R-13	R-13	R-19	R-4	R-11	R-4
5	x			R-38	R-30	R-13	R-11	R-13	R-4	R-11	R-4
5		x	x	R-38	R-38	R-13	R-13	R-19	R-4	R-11	R-4
6	x			R-22	R-22	R-11	R-11	R-11	(C)	R-11	R-4
6		x	x	R-38	R-30	R-13	R-11	R-13	R-4	R-11	R-4

Seal all penetrations in the building envelope

Be aware of any penetrations in the building envelope where air might escape directly to the outside. The uppermost ceiling in a house is the Swiss cheese of the building envelope. Every time your electrician or plumber drills a hole in the top wall plate for a wire or a pipe, the envelope is breached. If the ceiling is to be insulated, all of those penetrations should be sealed with spray foam insulation (see the photos on p. 17).

Besides sealing the drilled holes, seal the wall-to-ceiling intersection as well, an often overlooked culprit for envelope breaches. In addition, it is now common to foam holes drilled laterally between joist bays or stud bays. The theory is that sealing these holes also minimizes possible air movement from bay to bay within a wall or ceiling.

Types of Insulation

Before you decide how best to insulate your home, here's a brief look at the major types of insulation. The best way to think of those different types of insulation is in terms of how the insulation is installed. The three basic types are blown-in (cellulose), sprayed-in (foam), and fiberglass that is placed into the framing.

Blown-in insulation

As its name implies, blown-in insulation is shot into the cavities between framing members under moderate pressure (see the top photo on p. 20). As the insulation is blown into each cavity, it fills up all of the air spaces, making it a very efficient way of insulating. Blown-in insulation is also a very popular way of

The intersection between wall framing and ceiling framing is notorious for air leaks, so run a bead of foam along this intersection.

Sealing the areas where pipes or wires pass through studs or joists within an insulated space cuts down air movement from bay to bay.

insulating an attic floor. Most often blown-in insulation is cellulose made from recycled ground-up newspaper, giving it points with the "green building" community. But installing this type of insulation requires special skills and equipment, so I'd leave it to the pros.

Sprayed-in insulation

Sprayed-in or spray-foam insulation is the most efficient option. It is applied in a liquid state that rapidly foams and expands to fill the frame cavity. If applied correctly, spray foam also forms a solid air and moisture barrier. But spraying in foam insulation is a highly technical task and again, should be done only by an experienced professional. In addition to special skills, it requires special equipment, clothing, and safety measures. It's also the most expensive of the three options.

Fiberglass insulation

The most common insulating material in American homes is fiberglass. Fine glass fibers are spun into fluffy layers that resemble cotton candy. Fiberglass insulation comes either in long rolls or bundles of batts that are precut to shorter lengths. Fiberglass insulation is manufactured in different thicknesses to

Cellulose being blown into ceiling.

Insulation being sprayed in.

create different R-values, and it is available in different widths to fit between framing members.

Fiberglass insulation is available "faced," with an integral vapor barrier attached to one side. That vapor barrier has flanges along both edges that staple to the framing. Fiberglass is also available unfaced, without a vapor barrier.

Installing Fiberglass Insulation

Okay, you're finally ready to install the insulation that you've purchased. When the delivery truck drops off the load, sort the insulation by thickness and by whether or not it is faced with a vapor barrier. As closely as possible, put the insulation into the areas where it will be installed, but don't start cutting open bundles or rolls quite yet. Make sure you're wearing your protective gear, especially a long-sleeve shirt and a dust mask.

Insulating the ceilings

It really doesn't matter whether you start with the walls or ceilings. I like to get the overhead work done first, so I start with the ceilings. But there are similar challenges with every area. If you're using batts for all the areas (as shown here), begin by cutting open a bundle of batts. Open the bundles only as you need them. To take up less space, manufacturers greatly compress fiberglass insulation at the factory. When the packaging is cut, the batts expand in thickness to several times their packaged size.

Fiberglass insulation comes either as batts (precut lengths shown here) or in rolls. Fiberglass is also available with or without an integral vapor barrier attached to one side.

Batts or Rolls

Batts are cut either to 93 in., to fit between the plates on 8-ft. walls, or to 48-in. lengths, although some cutting is always required. With rolls, every piece has to be cut. When I was a contractor, batts were not always available in the configurations I needed, but today most professional installers prefer batts to rolls.

Fiberglass insulation is available as either batts (precut lengths) or as rolls that need to be cut to length.

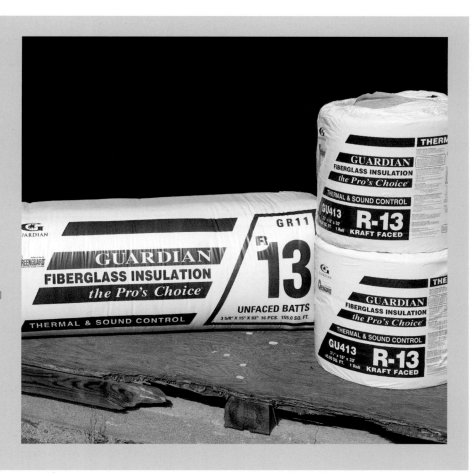

Pros

Installing fiberglass insulation does not require any special tools or skills. You cut it with a utility knife and install by stapling the edge of the vapor barrier to the studs. The installation process goes very quickly, and virtually every lumber store or home center in America sells fiberglass insulation in any configuration you need.

Cons

Working with fiberglass insulation is an itchy proposition: The stuff is very irritating to skin, eyes, and lungs. Over the years, I got so sensitive to fiberglass insulation that if I dared work without a dust mask—no matter how small the job—my lungs became inflamed and I started coughing immediately. The solution, however, is simple: Wear protective clothing (long pants and long-sleeve shirt), goggles, and a good dust mask. If taking these precautions turns you off, then consider having a professional install the insulation.

TOOLS NEEDED

- Utility knife
- Stapler (electric, hammer tacker, or staple gun)
- Putty knife

MATERIALS NEEDED

- Insulation (batts and/or rolls)
- Styrofoam rafter-bay vents
- Staples
- Protective equipment: paper suit, dust mask, goggles or safety glasses

Install Styrofoam® ventilation channels first

Proper ventilation and air circulation in your attic is crucial to the health and maintenance of your home. Typically, vents in the soffits allow fresh air into the attic via the spaces between the rafters. The air then rises and exits through a vent at the roof ridge. Improperly installed ceiling insulation can block those spaces and impede air circulation, which in turn can create a whole host of problems, from condensation and mold to ice dams and even failure of the roof sheathing. So before the insulation goes in, it's imperative to create a permanent path for attic air circulation.

Fortunately, the solution—plastic ventilation channel—is inexpensive, low-tech, and easy to install. These U-shaped channels are stapled to the underside of the sheathing and maintain an open air space between the soffit and the attic space. The channels are available in a variety of lengths from 2 ft. to 6 ft. and are made to fit the width between rafters. To add sufficient ventilation for most non-cathedral (flat) ceilings, 2-ft. or 3-ft. lengths are fine, depending on the pitch of the roof. (The shallower the roof pitch, the longer the ventilation channel needs to extend past the level of the insulation.)

Installing the channels is easy. Place a section of channel in each rafter bay. Make sure that it extends beyond the outer edge of the wall plate below (see the left photo on p. 24). Then fasten the channel to the underside of the roof sheathing with staples every 6 in. or so. Each rafter bay, including the narrow ones, should get a section of channel. For narrow bays, slit a length of channel lengthwise to the proper width (see the right photo on p. 24).

Cutting fiberglass insulation

Whether you decide to go with batts or rolls, you'll need to make cuts in the insulation. The fastest and easiest way to cut through insulation is with a utility knife. Keeping a sharp blade in the knife is very important, especially when you have to cut through paper facing as well as the insulation itself.

When I had to install fiberglass insulation as a contractor, I always set up a cutting station on the floor (see the sidebar on p. 26). But I recently had a chance to work with Bruce Trott, a professional installer who gave me a completely different perspective and approach. Cutting fiberglass slices up any surface under the insulation, so you need some sort of sacrificial surface to cut on. With the cutting station, a plywood scrap keeps the floor sheathing from getting damaged. But I was amazed to see Bruce just hold the batt against the nearest stud and slice away. This method saves you (and your knees) from having to

Styrofoam vent channel provides clear air passage from the eaves past the insulation in each bay. This clear space is crucial to keep the attic spaces ventilated.

Don't forget vent channel in the narrow bays. Use a utility knife to cut the channel lengthwise.

bend down every time a cut is needed. It also lets you cut the batt right where you're putting it to save extra steps. And the drywall covers any slices in the studs.

The cutting process is simple. First determine the length you'll need. With fiberglass batts, exact measurements aren't necessary. In fact, Bruce said that he tries to add ½ in. or so to his cuts so that adjacent pieces fit together snugly without compressing the insulation. So first you pull out your measuring tape, right? Wrong! Just hold the batt up to the section you're fitting and pinch the insulation between your thumb and finger at the length you need. Then place the batt against a stud face and slice across. If the insulation is faced, have the paper side toward you so that you cut through it first. After slicing through the paper, continue slicing through the insulation. With a sharp blade, it should take only one or two passes to cut all the way through. If you're cutting along the length of a batt, such as for a narrow joist bay, cut through the top half of the paper first, then cut through the insulation on that half. When that's cut through, flip the piece end for end and cut through the rest. By the way, if using a sharp utility knife along the narrow edge of a stud makes you nervous, use the broad face of a jack stud in a nearby doorway. As we get to more particular cutting tasks, I'll describe them in greater detail.

Start with the ends of the bays

The first pieces of insulation to go into the ceiling are short pieces cut to fit over the wall plates at the end of each bay. These pieces are installed with the vapor barrier facing down toward the top of the plate. Count the bays in the section that you're working and cut that number of pieces. The plates are 2×6, but cut the pieces to about 8-in. lengths so that you have good coverage. To put them in place, use a rolling motion so that the vapor barrier "rolls" onto the plate and extends to the middle of the furring strip where the ceiling meets the wall (see the top photo on p. 27). Make sure the pieces are not compressed but are fluffed to their natural state.

To cut insulation to length, pinch the batt with a thumb and finger. Then hold it against a nearby stud and cut through. If the insulation is paper-faced, cut through the facing first.

To cut insulation lengthwise, pinch the width and cut from the top about halfway down the batt. Then flip the batt over and cut from the other end.

Set Up a Cutting Station

If you decide to use rolls of insulation, then cutting against the edge of a stud might be awkward. As with batts, rolls of insulation are compressed at the factory. When you cut the tape or packaging that holds the roll together, it wants to expand to its working thickness. In doing so, it will unroll itself—in a dramatic fashion. So before you cut open the first roll, set up a cutting station.

   Place a piece of scrap plywood about 3 ft. from a framed interior wall as a cutting board. Tack the scrap to the subfloor to keep it from sliding around. Place the roll between the cutting board and the wall with the end coming out at the bottom and snip the retaining tape or packaging. Set up properly, the interior wall should keep the roll from unrolling (see the top right photo). Unlike cutting against a stud, the facing of the insulation will be pointing down (toward the floor). To cut through the insulation quickly and efficiently, compress the insulation with a 2× cutting guide and run your knife along the 2× to slice through. You should be able to cut through the insulation as well as the paper facing in one stroke.

   If you're making a number of repeat cuts, such as for stud bays in a wall, draw a line across the cutting board and measure the length you need from the line. Now tack another 2× scrap to the floor as a stop block at the length you need. Now it's just a matter of pulling the tail of the roll out until in bumps into the stop block and cutting as many lengths as you need.

If you're using rolls of fiberglass, set up a cutting station against an interior wall consisting of a cutting board and a stop block set at the proper measurement (top). The wall keeps the fiberglass from unrolling, and the moveable stop block lets you cut multiple pieces to the same length (above). Compress the insulation with a 2× cutting guide before slicing through.

The insulation goes in

Whether installing insulation from a roll or from batts (as is shown in this chapter), you'll need to cut the insulation to fit. Here is one place where rolls might make sense, as they allow you to work with long uninterrupted pieces. That said, keeping long lengths of insulation in place in the joist bays while stapling can be frustrating if you're working alone.

In my book *Framing a House*, you can read my argument for putting furring strips on ceilings, which is a practice found only in small areas of this country. Furring strips help flatten the ceiling, increase the nailing for the drywall, and create a chase for the systems. The code even recognizes furring as adding lateral rigidity to the house. Another advantage to this practice is supporting the insulation overhead. Regardless of whether or not you have furring strips on your ceilings, feed insulation into each joist bay. When the insulation is up between the joists, grab the end of the facing and pull the batt over until it butts against the insulation pieces that you installed above the plates. Tuck the facing above the furring strip or up on top of the plate to ensure good contact with the end pieces. Pull the facing down to the bottom edges of the joists and make it as smooth as possible across the joist bay. The insulation should fit snugly against the joists on both sides. Finally, staple the paper flange to the joists every foot or so.

Working with longer pieces of insulation makes it difficult to make sure the ends of the joist bays are filled. Instead, start with shorter pieces and "roll" them into position so the paper facing rests on top of the wall plate.

Feed the insulation carefully into each joist bay (above right), then grip the facing and pull it back into position against the adjacent piece (right). This motion ensures that the insulation is expanded fully and is in full contact with the sides of the joists.

Always Use a Sharp Blade

Change the blade on your utility knife at the first sign of dullness. A sharp blade is imperative for cutting cleanly through the insulation and the paper face.

Ceiling details

I try to make the ends of the batts land over a furring strip so they are supported. If you don't have furring strips, I recommend taping the butt joint between sections. Packing tape works fine for this application. Look for any hidden spaces and make sure they get insulated. Framers normally put up 2× nailers along gable walls to catch the ends of the furring strips or the edges of the ceiling drywall. Those nailers create hidden little voids over the wall plates that can be easy to overlook. For 2×6 walls, cut 6-in.-wide pieces of

insulation and fill those voids, again with the paper facing down against the plate.

With all framed bays—joists, studs, or rafters—you need to work around plumbing and electrical obstacles. Wires can be found just about anywhere and going in just about any direction in framed bays. The best advice is to detail the insulation so that the wires go through the insulation without creating a void and without compressing the insulation. (I go into greater detail about detailing around wires in the section on insulating walls on p. 35.) If there is slack in the wires, gently pull them down even with the bottom of the joist, letting the insulation go over the top. If the wires pass through the middle of the joist bay, you can split the insulation, putting half the thickness above and half below the wire. Where a wire starts out below the joist then rises to feed a fixture, make a small slit in the facing and the insulation for the wire then let the insulation fill in and wrap neatly around the wire. When one or more wires go straight across a joist bay, a good option is to create a seam between batts at the

Be sure to fill all hidden voids, such as these spaces behind 2× nailers. Any uninsulated part of the house is a potential area for energy loss and poor performance.

wire. If you use this option, just make sure the adjacent batts fit together snugly around the wire.

Some of the toughest obstacles you encounter while insulating a ceiling are fixtures for recessed lighting and exhaust vents. These fixtures can generate heat and sufficient clearance must be maintained around them for fire safety. This clearance space basically translates into a void (and therefore a weak link) in the insulation layer unless you construct an elaborate insulated enclosure. The best solution is to purchase

and install ceiling fixtures with an insulation-contact or IC rating clearly labeled on the fixture (see the top left photo on p. 30). IC fixtures allow you to insulate right up to the fixture. These fixtures might cost a little more up front, but that extra cost is minimal compared to the long-term energy losses you'll otherwise have to deal with.

To work around an IC-rated fixture, start by measuring and cutting a batt so that one end lines up with the far end of the fixture. Now hold the piece

Where a wire goes up on the side of a joist to feed a fixture, make a small slit in the facing as well as in the insulation (left). Then tuck the insulation around the wire and complete the detail by stapling both sides of the slit to the joist (bottom left).

Instead of slitting or separating the insulation for a wire, simply end that section at the wire. The end of the next section encloses the wire as the pieces butt together.

Look for a label on ceiling fixtures indicating that insulation can be installed without clearance space. The label is called IC, or insulation contact.

To fit insulation around an IC fixture, first measure and cut the length to end at the edge of the fixture.

against the ceiling and pinch the measurement for the near end of the fixture. Make a slit across the paper close to where the fixture falls side-to-side in the bay. Hold up each side next to the fixture and make slits for the width of the fixture. Again err on the side of making the cutout slightly small so that it fits snugly around the fixture. When the paper is removed, carve into the fiberglass, removing what you need for the insulation to fit around the fixture. Feed the section of insulation carefully into the joist bay and gently pull the insulation into place so that it fits evenly around the fixture without being compressed. The next batt section then butts against the excavated piece to create continuous insulation around the fixture.

Measure to the other side of the fixture (above left) and make a slit in the paper face (left).

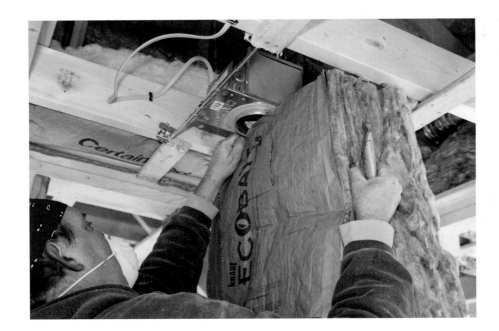

Remove the rectangular piece of facing and cut a cube out of the insulation to fit around the fixture housing (below). Last, feed the piece of insulation into place and gently pull the facing down around the fixture, making sure the insulation above stays intact (bottom).

Now measure the area on either side of the facing and make corresponding slits.

If you've already installed recessed lighting fixtures that do not have an IC rating, the best solution is to make an insulation "dam" out of wood or sheet metal to ensure that proper clearance is maintained. Along with the fixture there should be information supplied by the manufacturer to indicate just how much clearance space is required. Be sure to create clearance over the top of the fixture as well. In some situations, the best solution might be to fabricate a box with a piece of fire-code drywall over the top.

Insulating around a bathroom exhaust fan presents a similar set of problems, with the added challenge of the duct itself. The easiest approach is to cut the length so the batt ends at the edge of the unit where the duct attaches. Then it's just a matter of cutting out the insulation to go around the duct. This time, the void for the duct is cut from the top or the insulation side, leaving the facing intact along with a few inches of

insulation to fit under the duct. Flexible duct needs a little length to make the bend upward without kinking so make the cutout as wide as the diameter of the duct, but 2 in. or 3 in. longer than that diameter. When you push the batt into position, the duct should follow the void upward and then over the top of the adjacent batts.

Fitting insulation around the rest of the exhaust fan housing is the same detail as for the lighting fixture. First cut the paper facing and then carve out enough of the insulation to go around the housing. When you move the batt into position, separate the insulation to go above and below the wire to the fixture. Carefully pull the narrow tab of facing into position next to the fixture. When the facing is in place around the fixture, reach through the empty joist bay next door and make sure the batt meets its neighbor and that insulation fills all the voids around the fixture.

████████████

To fit insulation around an exhaust-fan duct, cut a void out of the top of the insulation (top) and then push the insulation into place with the duct fitting into the void (left).

ESSENTIAL TECHNIQUE

Insulating around a Chimney

Chimneys present a challenge because they require clearance to combustible materials. For masonry chimneys, that clearance is 2 in. This means the framed chase around a masonry chimney has to be at least 2 in. from the brick or block. That space can be filled with noncombustible insulation, such as unfaced fiberglass. Run the faced insulation up to the chase framing and then cut strips of unfaced insulation to go between the chimney and the chase.

Check with your building official to make sure this insulation detail is approved in your area. Insulated metal chimneys can vary depending on the manufacturer, so check the specs of your particular chimney before insulating around it.

Last, chimneys should be air-sealed so warm air cannot pass around the chimney and into the attic. This step may best be done at the drywalling stage by filling the gap between the chimney and the edge of the drywall with high-temperature caulk.

Cathedral ceilings

Putting insulation in a cathedral ceiling is a lot like insulating a flat ceiling. However, the process is complicated because the insulation has to fill most of the volume of the rafter bay. In order to keep the rafter bays adequately ventilated, plastic ventilation channel has to be installed the whole length from the eaves to the ridge, or from the eaves past any flat ceiling that might intersect with the cathedral ceiling. As with the ventilation channel on a flat ceiling, extend the first length past the top wall plate and staple the flanges to the underside of the roof sheathing. Butt a second section of channel to the first and continue up the rafter bay. If the cathedral ceiling ends at a flat ceiling, keep adding sections until the ventilation channel extends well past the flat ceiling. Err on the side of too long rather than too short for this detail. Better to use a little extra channel than to have the airway obstructed

For the adjacent piece, cut out the facing and make a void to fit around the fan housing. When putting the piece into position, separate the layers to go around the wires (top), then carefully lead the tab into position to complete the insulation layer around the housing (above).

For cathedral ceilings, ventilation channel has to be installed along the entire length of the cathedral portion of the ceiling. Here the cathedral ceiling intersects with a flat ceiling, so the channel extends past the flat ceiling insulation.

by the flat ceiling insulation. If the cathedral area extends to the peak of the ceiling or to the ridge, measure and cut the top section to length and staple it in place.

Install the fiberglass insulation as you did before, with the vapor barrier facing toward the room. To make installation easier, start the first course of batts at the lowest furring strip, or about 18 in. from the top of the wall. This strategy lets you configure the bottom end of each bay with a smaller, easier-to-handle piece. Always start by slipping the batt further up the rafter bay. Then pull the batt down into position. Again, staple the vapor barrier flanges to the lower faces of the rafters. The bottom pieces finish the bay and then extend over the wall plate. For the length of these

pieces, measure from the first course to the bottom edge of the cathedral ceiling, and then add 8 in. or so to cover the wall plate. Slit the paper facing 8 in. from the end. Now feed the insulation into place. The slit in the facing lets you pull ceiling insulation into place separately from the insulation that goes over the plates.

Detail around recessed lighting fixtures and wires the same as you did in the flat ceiling. The cathedral ceiling shown here was framed with short sections of

Keep the bottom pieces smaller so they are easier to get into place. A slit in the facing helps the piece make the transition to the wall plate.

To install insulation in a cathedral ceiling, insert the batt above where it's going and pull it down and into position.

Slipping Insulation into Stud Bays

The inside faces of the studs might be rough and could snag the insulation, keeping it from fluffing out fully. If a piece of insulation does not slip easily into its stud bay, run a putty knife along the edges so the piece expands fully.

2×4 nailers to attach the bottom furring strip. Instead of just stuffing the insulation between the nailers, make cutouts on either side to fit neatly around the nailers. For this ceiling area, starting the first course of batts at the first furring strip also allowed the course above to be completed with a half batt. A little forward thinking saved a lot of extra cutting as well as wasted material. The top course of the cathedral ceiling insulation extends past the intersection of the flat ceiling, and the flat ceiling insulation then butts into it. This flat ceiling area had a peculiar detail—the electrical box for the smoke detector. Here we put the batt into place and then cut out the paper facing along with a shallow area of fiberglass. We then wrapped the facing around the sides of the box and stapled it into place.

Insulating walls

With the ceilings finished, you can now turn to the walls. So far in this chapter we've used batts instead of rolls, and we continue with batts for the walls. Installation is essentially the same, except you're working in a vertical configuration. Notice that we're using unfaced insulation for this part. We deal with the vapor barrier on the walls a little later on.

The stud bays here were slightly shorter than the standard length of the batts, so we pushed the batts up against the top plate and left them long at the bottom. It's easier to trim the bottoms all at once when the batts are in place. As with the joist bays on the ceiling, if a stud bay is more than an inch narrower than the full width, you need to cut that section to width as

In this ceiling, 2× nailers were installed in every other joist bay. To keep the insulation from being bunched up between them, cut voids on both sides to go around the nailers.

For an electrical box in the ceiling, cut out the facing and a shallow layer of insulation for the box. Then pull the facing down around the box.

To install batts in the walls, start by pushing the batt all the way to the top. Note that this insulation is unfaced. The vapor barrier will be added later.

well. To trim a longer wall batt to width, first hold it up to the target stud bay and pinch the width with your thumb and forefinger. Place the batt against a stud (the doubled 2× framing around a window or door is best) and cut through the insulation from the top. When you've cut about halfway down the batt, flip it over and finish the cut from the other end. Install the trimmed section the same as with the other bays, from the top down.

Go back and trim the bottoms of the batts by running your utility knife along the bottom edge of the wall plate. Then tuck the bottoms neatly into place in the stud bays. Now measure, cut, and install the shorter pieces, such as for above and below windows. If the framer did a good job, those lengths should be consistent. Next, fill in any oddball areas with leftover scraps (you have been saving your scraps, right?), again taking care not to compress the insulation. Note that with unfaced insulation the batts are held in the stud bays by friction alone, without staples.

To trim long lengths to a narrower width, first determine the width and, starting from the top, cut down to roughly the middle of the length (top). Then turn the batt upside down and cut the rest of the way, again from the top (right).

Install all the batts with the bottom ends sticking out. Then go back and trim them all at once.

For shorter pieces under a window, measure the length of one and then cut as many as you need at one time.

Smaller odd-shaped areas can be filled in with scraps. Just be sure that the spaces are filled completely without compressing the insulation.

Detailing around wires and boxes

In an insulator's perfect house, all the joist bays and stud bays would be the same width and length and there would be no obstacles to work the insulation around. Unfortunately, that perfect house would have no windows, electricity, or plumbing—not my idea of perfect! So you have to make the insulation fit around the obstacles in the walls.

The most common obstacles in walls are wires and electrical boxes. When you encounter a wire crossing a stud bay, separate the batt into two layers up or down to the level of the wire (short sections of insulation can be separated completely). Fortunately, fiberglass insulation is made of thin layers that combine to create the specified thickness—sort of like a cross between cotton candy and phyllo dough—so splitting it into two layers is an easy task. Tuck the back layer of the batt into place behind the wire and then push the front layer into place against the back layer. This way, the wire essentially goes through the insulation and the insulation is not compressed.

To insulate around wires, separate the batt into two layers (top right). Feed the first layer into place behind the wire (right). Then press the outside layer into place (far right).

Where there is an electrical box in a stud bay, again separate the batt into layers and tuck the back layer behind the box. If the insulation is unfaced, just cut out a cube of the front layer slightly smaller than the box and tuck the insulation around the box. Make short diagonal slits from the corners of the cube to allow the insulation to wrap around the box more easily. If the insulation is faced, carefully cut the paper facing, again slightly smaller than the box, and cut out the same cube from the front layer of insulation with diagonal slits through the facing as well as the insulation.

One-piece plastic vapor barrier

We chose unfaced insulation for the walls, but that doesn't sidestep the need for a vapor barrier. Instead of the barrier being attached to the insulation (as it was in the ceilings), we will cover the entire insulated wall with a plastic film. This strategy is quicker than having to staple the facing on both sides of each individual batt. It also forms a more complete and uninterrupted barrier than you'd get with faced insulation. Use a fairly heavy plastic (6 mil) to minimize ripping and stretching.

Start by unrolling the plastic along the wall. (Rolls of plastic usually come with the width doubled over at least twice for ease of handling.) Pinch the length you need and unroll the plastic a little more so that you're cutting on the subfloor and not on the roll. If you keep

To insulate around electrical boxes in a wall, cut out a small rectangular void in the outer layer. If you make the void slightly smaller than the box, the insulation will make a snug wrap around the box.

To create a vapor barrier over unfaced insulation, first unroll a plastic sheet to the proper length and cut the sheet parallel to the roll.

Insulating around Wires

Instead of splitting the batt into two layers, just make a slit about halfway through the insulation from the back at the height of the wire, leaving the paper face intact. Then tuck the wire into the slit so the insulation fills in around the wire.

Unfold the sheet and start in one corner (top), stapling both sides of the corner securely. Then lead the factory edge of the plastic sheet along the top plate, stapling it as you go (above).

the plastic stretched tight between the roll and your cut, you can make your cut parallel to the roll to keep it straight and fairly square. When you've cut all the way through, staple one upper corner to the framing, letting a factory edge of the plastic follow the top plate. Staple the corner securely with three or four staples on each leg of the corner. Continue across the wall, stretching the plastic with one hand and stapling with the other. Drive a staple above each stud.

When the top edge is secure, start in the middle of the wall, pull down on the sheet, and drive a staple into a stud. Work from the middle toward each side, pulling the plastic tight both down and to the side by grabbing it a couple of feet from where you're stapling. Pull the plastic tight at each end and secure it to the end studs. When the plastic sheet is tight across the entire wall, go back and drive staples into each stud every foot or so. Finish by stapling the sheet to the bottom plate, and then cut off the excess at the edge of the bottom plate. At this point, don't worry about cutting the plastic around the window or electrical boxes. That can be left to the drywallers, and the plastic offers a modicum of protection in the meantime.

When the top edge is stapled, smooth the sheet down in the middle and staple it to a stud face. Working in both directions, grab the sheet, stretch it taut, and staple it in place.

Staple off the entire sheet except for the bottom edge. Trim the excess off the bottom before stapling that edge.

Basement ceilings

Back in the 1980s and 1990s, the only basement ceilings we insulated were in houses that had no furnace or boiler, such as those with electric heat. That way warmth from these heating devices would rise and warm the floor above. But then came high-efficiency units that gave off little or no heat (the heat from older boilers was basically wasted energy).

Today there seems to be two different approaches: either insulate the basement ceiling and keep the basement as an unconditioned space, or insulate the basement walls (inside and out) and leave the ceiling uninsulated. The first strategy is best when the basement is not being finished. Insulating the basement walls is preferable if the basement is to be used as living space. If you are on the fence about which strategy to use, contact your local utility company or a home energy consultant to get their recommendation.

Insulating basement walls is a whole topic unto itself, so let's stick to insulating the basement ceiling. Start by cutting and placing short pieces of insulation between the joists and against the rim joist. These short sections are a great opportunity to use up scraps or cut-off pieces. Completely fill each bay above the sill plate and against the rim. If you're using faced

Stapling Faced Insulation

Instead of a solid sheet of plastic for a vapor barrier, faced insulation can be used in the stud bays (see the photo at right) With the ceiling insulation, the vapor barrier was stapled to the sides of the 2× framing, a method called "inset" stapling. But there is another school of thought for stapling insulation to the studs. As a contractor, I always stapled the insulation flanges to the narrow edges of the studs facing into the room, a process called "face" stapling (see the drawing below). So which method is right? A few years back I posed this question in *Fine Homebuilding's* Q&A column to Gene Leger, a home energy consultant from New Hampshire. He pointed out that inset stapling has a number of drawbacks. First, inset stapling compresses the edges of the batts, lowering their effectiveness. Next, it creates an air space instead of allowing the batt to fill the stud cavity fully. The air space and the potential for air movement also reduces the effectiveness of the insulation. Finally, and most important, inset stapling creates a potential fire hazard. The paper face of insulation is flammable, but the code allows it to be used in a concealed space such as a stud bay if the face is in direct contact with the drywall. Inset stapling reduces the amount of that contact. By the way, manufacturers allow both methods of stapling, so the choice is yours.

You can use faced insulation for walls. Just be sure to staple the facing securely to the studs.

Face Stapling Versus Side Stapling Insulation

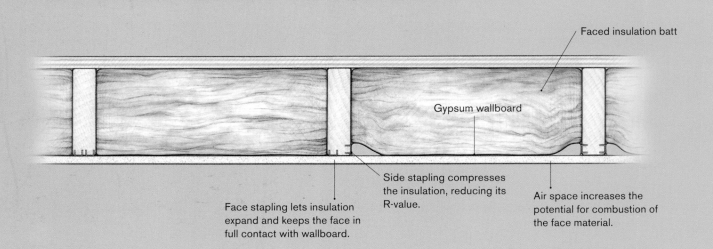

Faced insulation batt

Gypsum wallboard

Face stapling lets insulation expand and keeps the face in full contact with wallboard.

Side stapling compresses the insulation, reducing its R-value.

Air space increases the potential for combustion of the face material.

insulation, the paper should be toward the inside of the joist bay. The rim-joist pieces should fit snugly into place without compressing the insulation.

In the main part of the ceiling, the batts then butt against the rim-joist insulation. If you're using faced insulation, the paper should be installed toward the underside of the floor above. Each successive batt of insulation should butt against the previous one. As before, place the batt into the bay and then pull it toward the adjacent batt. Detail around plumbing and electrical obstacles as you did in the ceilings before, except that the paper facing stays intact on the top side of the insulation.

As you might expect, your biggest enemy with installing basement ceiling insulation is gravity. To hold the insulation in place, use insulation supports, known in the business as "lightning rods." These supports are about the thickness of a coat hanger and slightly longer than the width of the joist bay. Each rod is pushed up against the insulation in a slightly bowed position with the ends wedged against the inside faces of the joists (see the photo on p. 44). The biggest drawback to using these supports is that they compress the insulation slightly as they bow upward, which lessens the R-value of the insulation. So push the rods up with just enough pressure to contact the underside of the insulation.

When insulating a basement ceiling, install the insulation with the vapor barrier facing toward the floor above. Note that I-joist framing requires wider insulation.

Insulating a Basement Wall

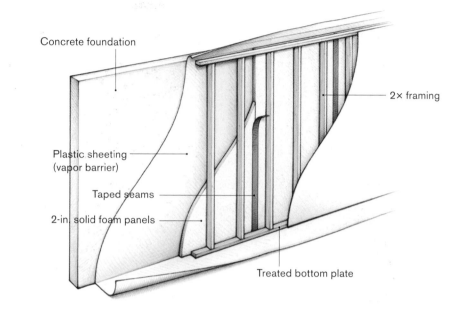

Concrete foundation

2× framing

Plastic sheeting (vapor barrier)

Taped seams

2-in. solid foam panels

Treated bottom plate

Lightweight wires called lightning rods wedge between the
joists to keep the insulation in place. Push them up lightly to
keep the insulation from compressing.

Insulating between I-Joists

Insulation is manufactured in widths to fit between conventional framing: 15 in. wide for 16-in. o.c. framing. The
webs or vertical components of I-joists are much narrower,
so 15-in.-wide insulation will not fill an I-joist bay. If your
house is framed with I-joists, be sure to specify full-width
insulation (16 in. wide for 16-in. o.c. framing) for those
applications.

Insulating the walls around a tub/shower unit is a great way to deaden the sound of water beating against the unit's fiberglass walls.

Insulating for sound

In addition to its ability to inhibit the movement of heat through a wall or ceiling, fiberglass insulation is also great for deadening sound. I've seen some owners go to the extreme of insulating all the walls in their master bedrooms for silence and privacy. Home theaters are another place where insulation is used for sound deadening. The most common sound-deadening application is around a fiberglass tub/shower unit. While these bathing fixtures are conve-

nient, they can sound like a metal roof in a rainstorm when the water is running. Insulating around these units helps to keep the noise from reaching nearby rooms. The insulation around a shower needs only to be the thickness of the walls (usually 2×4) and just needs to fill the stud bays around the unit itself. Use unfaced insulation and fill the bays from top plate to bottom plate.

Drywall

Drywall revolutionized residential construction. Most of us just don't think about it. You walk into a house and the walls are flat and smooth—enough said. But in most houses built since the middle of the 20th century we owe those smooth, flat walls to drywall. This product is deceptively simple. It's gypsum material wrapped with paper and it installs quickly and easily. The paper finish readily accepts paint, so it's an interior decorator's dream, and it also offers a measure of fire resistance (specially formulated fire-code drywall should be used for certain specified applications, such as garages).

When I was building houses in the 1980s, drywall was the most frustrating part of any job I undertook. I always tried to make everything fit just so, and ended up cutting and recutting pieces. And finishing the drywall made my hair fall out! Then I got to work with drywall specialist Myron Ferguson with *Fine Homebuilding* magazine. First of all, Myron's approach to drywall was almost serene. He did write the book on it, after all (*Drywall 4th Edition*, Taunton Press 2012). Myron always worked steadily and methodically, and his work turned out beautifully with minimal mess. My drywall technique will never be as good as Myron's, but I have come to enjoy the Zen of drywall.

Loading Drywall into the House

On one of the first houses I did on my own, we had the drywall delivery truck arrive and just leave all the drywall in the garage—not smart! We ended up muscling the sheets into the rooms, straining our young backs, and damaging the edges of the drywall as we went up stairs and around corners. We made that mistake only once. The next time we ordered drywall for a home, we went to a drywall-supply house. They arrived with a boom truck specially equipped to lift many sheets at a time. They also have a small army of

A boom truck is the fastest, safest, and easiest way to get drywall into a home. Most drywall-supply houses use these trucks to deliver their products.

SHOULD I TACKLE THIS MYSELF?

Pros

Hanging and finishing drywall is not rocket science. It takes a few basic and relatively inexpensive tools. Measurements don't have to be precise for cutting and fitting drywall, but taping and finishing is an acquired art. Once you get the hang of it, installing drywall can be a rewarding experience.

Cons

Until you've been a professional drywaller for a number of years, you'll never be able to work as quickly as a professional crew. If you do hire a crew, take the time to watch them in motion—you'll be amazed, and you'll learn by watching. These crews handle every phase of the process, letting you step back and save your energy for other finishing tasks. Drywall is heavy, so the installation process requires a lot of lifting. You might opt to have the pros install the board and you do the finishing. Drywall is a messy job; in fact, the mess itself might be enough to keep many wannabe drywallers away. Between the dust and getting drywall mud all over everything, I'm usually ready to hand the job over to a crew myself.

TOOLS NEEDED

- Utility knife with sharp blades
- 4-ft. drywall square
- Drywall rasp
- Screw gun with extra screw tips
- Drywall saw
- Drywall router
- Heavy-duty drill with mixing blade
- Mudpan
- Taping knives
- Joint knife

MATERIALS NEEDED

- Drywall sheets
- 1¼-in. drywall screws (large bucket)
- Drywall compound

ESTIMATING MATERIALS

Estimating drywall has a lot in common with the process you used for estimating insulation. It involves measuring the area you need to cover and knowing the type of drywall you need to use. For most homes, three basic types of drywall are needed: $\frac{1}{2}$-in.-thick standard drywall, $\frac{1}{2}$-in.-thick mold-resistant drywall (for moist areas such as bathrooms), and $\frac{5}{8}$-in.-thick fire-resistant drywall. The key to estimating is to know the lengths to order. Drywall comes 4 ft. wide and in even-foot lengths from 8 ft. to 16 ft. The longer the board you use, the fewer the seams to finish. But the boards also get heavier as they get longer, so before you order a load of 16-footers, make sure you've lined up help.

To estimate drywall, start in a room and go wall by wall and ceiling plane by ceiling plane. Round up the widths to the nearest 2 ft. In other words, if you have a wall that is 15 ft. long and 9 ft. high, you'll need three 16-ft. sheets to cover the wall. Again, look at interruptions in the wall. You might be able to get away with shorter sheets on either side of a window or door rather than cutting up a long sheet.

As you might have guessed, drywalling probably generates more waste than any other step in the building process. And the more funky angles for dormer cheeks and such, the more waste there tends to be. Even if you've decided to do your own drywall, have a pro come in and estimate the job as an exercise. A pro can go through a room in seconds and tell you how many sheets of each length is needed.

The most common drywall is the standard $\frac{1}{2}$-in.-thick variety. It is strong, fairly lightweight, and easy to work with.

Bathrooms and other moisture-prone areas require special drywall that is mold resistant. This type of drywall is usually a different color than regular drywall.

Drywall by itself has some fire-resistant qualities, but in some applications, such as garages, you must use $\frac{5}{8}$-in.-thick drywall that's specially formulated to resist fire for a longer period of time.

workers who are used to getting the drywall as close to where it will be used as possible. All you do is stay out of the way.

Windows and doors

Boom trucks are great, but the outside of your house is finished, and now you need to figure out how to get through the walls with the drywall. The answer is to remove windows. With the sashes removed, the boom truck just lifts the sheets to the window and workers do the rest. Garage doors are convenient for loading, as are front doors and sliding doors. If there is access, the boom truck can be repositioned on different sides of the house to load all areas of the home.

As the sheets come into the house, stack them on edge and arrange them in piles according to length. When the loading is finished, put the window sashes back in to make the house weathertight again. Remember that drywall is covered with paper that can absorb moisture. If sheets of drywall have to be stored temporarily in a space open to the weather, protect them by wrapping the load with plastic.

To get the sheets into areas of the home, especially on upper floors, remove the window sash and have the truck position the sheets just outside. Remember to protect the window sills from damage.

As the sheets come into a room, spread them around and arrange them by length for easy access.

If a sheet needs to be used in a width smaller than 4 ft., hold the measurement on the tape with your thumb and forefinger. Hold the blade of your utility knife against the tip of the tape and score along the length.

Cutting and Installing Drywall Sheets

I always enjoy the transformation that occurs as a house is built and finished. Some of the changes are dramatic, such as when the framed walls are raised into place. Drywall is just such a stage. You can literally start in the morning with exposed framing and insulation, and by the time you quit for the day the inside of the entire home has been transformed into a smooth, flat drywall surface. As a musician, I'm also keenly aware of the acoustics around me. With the installation of drywall, each room develops an echo or ring. The house is coming alive.

Score, snap, and slice

The first time I saw someone cut drywall I was amazed. I was ready for a tornado of dust and debris, but there was none of that. Here are the proper steps for measuring and cutting drywall.

When you've determined the size of the piece you'll need, go to the stack that is the closest to the right length. If you don't need the entire 4-ft. width, start by scoring the width you need. Hold the measurement on your tape with the thumb and forefinger on one hand and hold the blade of your utility knife against the end of the tape with your other hand. Starting at one end, score the length of the board, letting your measurement hand slide along the top edge of the board. (If the piece you need is closer to 4 ft. wide, hold the measurement of the waste piece instead. For example, for a piece 40 in. wide, hold the tape at 8 in.) Next, mark the length of the piece with the blade of the utility knife. Set your drywall square at that mark, hold the bottom of the square with your foot, and score across the width of the sheet.

To snap the piece, first apply pressure against the scored line for the width. The piece should snap along the line, leaving the paper on the opposite side intact and letting it act as a hinge. Holding the piece so that the two sides are at a slight angle to each other, stick the blade of your knife through the scored cut and

"No Need to Be So Precise!"

Those are the words of a seasoned homebuilder with whom I worked early on in my career. I hear those words and repeat them to myself every time I cut and install drywall. Carpenters routinely work to tolerances of $\frac{1}{32}$ in. or greater in their finish work. Working to close tolerances can slow you down and force you to shave pieces of drywall to get them to fit properly. The smallest increment you should consider with drywall is $\frac{1}{8}$ in., and usually $\frac{1}{4}$-in. tolerances are fine for your measurements. Remember, the seams get covered with tape and compound for 99 percent of all drywall installation, so repeat after me: "No need to be so precise!"

Now snap the sheet lengthwise. The paper on the other side of the drywall acts as a hinge. Holding the sheet with the cut slightly open, slice through the paper on the other side to separate the two pieces.

Next, snap the score you made across the sheet and cut through to separate the piece you need.

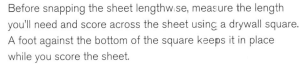

Before snapping the sheet lengthwise, measure the length you'll need and score across the sheet using a drywall square. A foot against the bottom of the square keeps it in place while you score the sheet.

slice through the paper on the other side, separating the two sides. Break the score you made for length and cut through that piece. Hit the rough edges of the cut with your drywall rasp to flatten them out and you're done.

The process of score, snap, and slice works for nearly every cut you make. For diagonal cuts, such as for the walls along a cathedral ceiling, measure and mark the triangular piece you need to *remove*. Measure the two sides and mark them out on the corner of a sheet. Now snap a chalkline between the two points and score along the line. Snap off the triangle and smooth the edge with a rasp. Later in this chapter I'll describe other methods of cutting that happen after the pieces are installed.

For diagonal cuts, measure and mark each leg of the triangle. Snap a chalkline between the marks. Carefully follow the snapped line with your utility knife to score the cut, and then finish the process as before.

The score, snap, and slice process can leave a ragged edge. Use a drywall rasp to smooth out the rough edges.

Install the sheets of drywall on the ceiling first while your arms are fresh. Plus the sheets on the wall will help support the edges of the ceiling.

Drywall's Tapered Edges

If you're familiar with drywall, you know that the long edges of each sheet taper to a thinner dimension. The paper wraps around these tapered edges as well. Whenever possible, these tapered edges should abut, creating space for the tape and compound. Avoid butting a tapered seam against a cut edge that is full thickness. These seams are almost impossible to fill and hide.

When you put the sheet in position, make sure it fits properly on all sides. Have your screw gun handy so you can grab it with one hand while holding the sheet with the other.

Install the ceilings first

As you hang the sheets of drywall in each room, there is no commandment that says you absolutely have to hang the ceilings first, but it makes sense for many reasons. First, it takes the most energy to lift sheets over your head and hold them there while you drive screws in, so why not do it when you're fresh and have the most strength? Second, when the ceilings are done first, the edges are supported by the sheets on the walls, minimizing chances for detachment along the edges.

If a room has extra-high ceilings, you need to work off of some sort of safe and substantial staging. Once a piece has been cut to length, pass the piece up to the person on the staging. Hold the piece in place and make sure you have your screw gun within reach. (By the way, with furring strips to screw into, you can run the sheets in either direction.) When the piece is in place, confirm that it fits properly along both edges, as well as against any neighboring sheet. While holding the sheet against the framing, grab your screw gun and drive five or six screws around the sheet to hold it in place. This is one instance where "using your head" can be taken literally. You need two hands to load most screw guns—one to hold the gun and one to put the screw in the tip. Push your noggin against the sheet to hold it in place, load the gun, and then drive the screw. When the sheet is held in place by the first few screws, your partner can let go and cut the next sheet while you drive the rest of the screws. Along the edge of the sheet, drive a 1¼-in. drywall screw at each framing member (or furring strip) and then one screw every 12 in. in the field.

One of the details to attend to while putting drywall on ceilings is to cut around electrical boxes and fixtures. The best time to do this task is after the sheet has been partially secured to the ceiling. Start by measuring from a point on an intersecting wall or a neighboring sheet to the center of the box. Attach the sheet with screws a good distance from the box (see the top photo on p. 54), then measure over to that point and plunge in with your drywall router. These tools turn at the speed of a router, but use a ⅛-in. drill

Drive five or six screws around the perimeter and in the field of the sheet to keep it in place. Then you can finish driving screws while your fellow crew member prepares the next piece.

ESSENTIAL TECHNIQUE

The Correct Depth for Drywall Screws

Screw guns come with a depth adjustment to ensure that the screws are driven to the correct depth. If the screw goes too deep, it breaks through the paper and there is a danger of the sheet tearing out around the screw. Too shallow and the screw head sticks out when you try to finish over it. With the proper setting, the screw dimples the surface of the drywall without breaking through.

Drive the drywall screws to the right depth. Too deep (left) and the screw can tear out through the paper; too shallow (center) and the screw head interferes with finishing. At the correct depth (right) the paper dimples slightly around the screw head.

ANOTHER WAY TO DO IT

Mechanical Drywall Lift

If help is at a premium and you end up hanging the ceilings by yourself, you can get a mechanical drywall lift that will save your back as well as your sanity. These helpful tools are available at most tool-rental outlets.

Electrical boxes are supposed to be flush with the drywall when finished. To cut out for them, first measure to the center of the box from a neighboring wall or drywall sheet (right). Attach the sheet away from the box location. Then plunge in with a drywall router and cut the perimeter of the box (below).

To bridge the corners of door openings for a stronger installation, let the drywall sheets extend right across the opening. Then go back and cut out the waste with a drywall router.

bit instead of a router bit. Cut from the center of the box out to the edge. When you hit the edge, lift the bit to get on the outside edge of the box. Then cut around the box, letting the box act as a guide for the bit.

Turn to the walls

If you've recruited a large number of helpers, one group can start on the walls if the ceilings in that area are done. In just about every case, walls get drywalled from the top down; in other words, the top pieces of drywall go in first. The pieces can generally go smack up to the ceiling and be screwed into place. If the wall angles up to the ceiling, measure and cut the angle as described on p. 51. Don't worry about piecing around framed openings such as doors at this point. Install the piece of drywall right over the door opening. This strategy is not only a faster way to install the drywall, but a solid piece of drywall around the top of the door also means less chance of cracking as the house settles. After the piece is screwed into place, go back with your drywall router and cut out the doorway. Another strategy is to cut the sides of the door opening with a drywall saw, leaving one line across the top that can be scored, snapped, and cut.

Now the pieces below can be put in by butting them up against the top piece. The same cutting strategy can be used around windows as well. In this case, the drywall has to fit around the extension jambs (the wood trim that connects the window to the trim). The inner edges of the extension jambs are flush with the surface of the drywall. Screw the drywall in place a couple of studs away from the window, letting the sheet extend over the corner of the window. Then let your drywall router follow outside the extension jambs to cut out the window.

When you install the bottom pieces on the walls, make them 1 in. or so short. The extra space will help to avoid any fussing to fit the piece in right, and it gives you space to use a foot lever to lift the piece into place (see the top photo on p. 56). This handy tool lets you use foot power to hold the drywall in place while you drive the screws.

It's also faster to cut out electrical boxes for switches and receptacles with the sheets in place. Remember that these boxes are installed to be flush

To work around a window, let the sheet extend over the corner. Fasten it a couple of feet away and then let the drywall router follow the outside edge of the extension jamb.

Another strategy for cutting out a door opening is to use a drywall saw on the two sides (left). Then score and slice across the top for a final cut (below).

Mark Off the Stud Locations

The wall studs don't always line up with the furring strips on the ceiling, especially if the ceiling is sloped. To avoid unnecessary holes from missed screws, mark the tops of the studs on the ceiling before you start.

Hang Bathrooms First

As we mentioned before, bathrooms and other moisture-prone areas get special drywall that resists mold growth. If you hang the bathrooms first, you can use leftover pieces of moisture-resistant board in other areas of the house.

Cut the bottom sheets on each wall a little short. Then use a handy foot lever to lift the sheet into place.

When the entire electrical box is behind the sheet, use the same strategy you used before on the ceilings. Measure over, plunge in the middle of the box, then move to the edge where you can follow the box's outside perimeter.

with the surface of the drywall, so they stick out ½ in. beyond the plane of the studs. This means that the boxes have to be cut out before the sheet sits completely on the framing. There are two basic scenarios for cutting boxes: Either the sheet completely covers the box, or it doesn't. The latter is the easiest because the location of the box is visible. In this instance, drive a few screws to hold the sheet in place. Then use your drywall router to follow the perimeter of the box before fastening the rest of the sheet. When the mating sheet is put in place, simply cut out the rest of the box.

The second scenario is the same as with the ceiling boxes we did earlier. Measure to the center of the box from an edge (such as a doorway or an adjacent sheet). When the sheet is in place, measure over and then plunge into the middle of the box with the drywall router. Cut over to one edge, then jump to the outside of the box and follow the perimeter as before. One note of caution: Keep the electrician happy and make sure the wires are pushed into the box far enough so that they don't get nicked by the router. Another place where electricians and drywallers cross paths is when bare wires are left in walls for things such as closet lights. In these cases, hang the drywall on the inside of the closet first. Then poke through from the back side with your drywall saw and stick the wire through.

The final tasks are filling in missing pieces such as window headers and mullion strips between sashes. If you've done a good job with the hanging and have used long lengths efficiently, these "patches" are the only places where two nontapered edges might butt. Make sure there are no hidden objects such as nail heads that could keep the two sides from meeting on exactly the same plane.

First Coat of Compound

Hanging the drywall can seem like a flurry of activity with dust and pieces of drywall flying around, and the noise of screw guns and routers. Taping and mudding (applying compound) can be downright serene by comparison. If you haven't done so already, throw out all the scraps of drywall and related debris. I like to give the floors a quick sweep as well. If there is one dropped screw in the whole place, the wheels from my staging will find it without a doubt.

Finishing the drywall happens in three progressive stages. The first stage covers all the seams with tape and compound and covers all the screw heads as well. Because taping is involved, the first stage is the most intensive. The next two stages are merely applying more compound in widening layers. Each progressive stage uses slightly different tools as well.

Prepare the compound

There are a bunch of different types of joint compound out on the market, including powdered varieties you mix with water. I know people who swear by various brands, or who mix a little of this and a little of that. I try to keep it simple and work with an all-purpose or multi-use compound. That said, I was taken a little aback when I saw drywall specialist Alain Fortin pour about ½ cup of dish detergent into a fresh 5-gal. bucket of compound before mixing it. He also added a little water to thin it out some. He claimed that the dish detergent made the compound go on more smoothly, and I've since read accounts of others who confirm his belief.

Regardless of whether you add anything to the compound or use it as-is from the bucket, it's imperative that you mix the compound thoroughly before using it. The best thing to use is a drywall mixing paddle chucked into a heavy-duty drill. There are many different configurations of mixing paddles, but

I'd go for a simpler (and usually cheaper) version. After Alain added the detergent and water, he stirred the compound a little by hand to avoid the liquid splashing out. Then he chucked the paddle into his drill and mixed it until it had the consistency of creamy icing. This process is repeated for every new bucket of compound you open. Without mixing, drywall compound is very hard to apply properly.

Add a little dishwashing liquid to the compound before mixing to make it spread more smoothly. Using a mixing paddle chucked into a heavy-duty drill, mix the compound thoroughly until it is the consistency of icing.

Lumps and Spills

One of the most frustrating parts of applying drywall compound is dealing with foreign objects in the compound. These things can range from small chunks of cured compound to insects or sawdust. You'll know right away because streaks or voids appear in the wake of your knife. If the object is apparent, stop immediately and dig it out. Most often these objects are chunks of compound, and the culprit is your knife. As you work, little bits of compound accumulate on the back side of the blade. If you don't scrape them off regularly, those pesky bits find their way into the fresh compound. Get in the habit of scraping the knife blade each time before dipping it back into the mudpan. Also, there will be times when you go the wrong direction with your knife and suddenly a large blob of compound plummets to the floor. Your frugal self will tempt you to scoop it up and reuse it: DON'T! Scrape it up so you don't step in it and track compound all over the place, but dispose of the contaminated compound in an old bucket or box. Once it's hit the floor or any surface other than your knife, it should not be used—period!

Ready to spread

For the first coat of compound, you'll need a drywall mudpan (a shallow metal trough) and a 6-in.-wide joint knife. Go for a good-quality knife with a fairly stiff blade. Using your knife as a scoop, fill your pan about ⅓ full. At this point you'll be using compound at a pretty good clip, so it's okay to leave the cover off the bucket. If you put the cover back on, watch for any little hard chunks of dried compound that might fall in.

When I did my first drywall work, sanding after each coat was a very time-consuming necessity. The better I got at applying compound, though, the less sanding I needed to do. My most recent drywall jobs have required no sanding. Honest! If you put the compound on properly, you won't have to sand between coats, but if you do, the sanding goes very quickly. The key is applying thin "tight" coats of compound and not overworking it. There are just a few major tasks in basic drywalling: covering screws, flat seams (tapered and not), inside corners, and outside corners. I'll cover these at each phase of the process.

So what is your plan of attack as you work through a room? You could do all the screws first, then all the flat seams, all the corners, and so on, but that would mean a lot of moving around and being in the same area more than once. Instead, work an area of the room. Most of the time you can blend later work with earlier work without a problem. You have a lot of ground to cover, so try to save steps by doing all the tasks in a given area before moving on. However, for the sake of explanation, I will describe one task at a time.

Covering screws

Let's start with the easy stuff first. If you did your own drywall hanging, you know that there are just short of a billion screws holding the drywall on—or so it seems. I've seen many people do each screw, one at a time. It takes two strokes: one to lay the compound on, the next to smooth it over. But why not do a whole row of screws at once? Start by dipping your knife into the mudpan and loading it with compound. Scrape the

The Drywall Hawk

Mudpans are inexpensive and hold a lot of compound, which lets you sling more mud without going back to the bucket. But there are other ways to hold compound for dispensing. One is to use a large joint knife to hold the compound in waiting, but the knife doesn't hold as much compound as the pan, and because the compound is not contained, you end up with plops of compound falling off the knife. A better alternative is the drywall hawk, which is a large square platform on a handle. The hawk holds a good quantity of material, and because of its size and shape, it's easier to use without leaving a mess.

mud off one side of the knife blade, leaving all the compound on the other side. In a quick, sideways motion, slather compound over a line of screws as far as you can reach comfortably on either side. Scrape the excess off the knife on the lip of the mudpan, and then go back over the line in the opposite direction and scrape off all the excess compound. Just two strokes: Apply the compound and take it back off. By the way, inevitably you'll hit a screw that is slightly too high. I carry a Phillips-head screwdriver in my back pocket to give the screw a slight turn so that it can be covered.

The key to this two-stroke process is the angle of the knife blade. Notice in the photos that the blade is nearly flat to apply the compound. But to take off the excess, the blade is almost perpendicular to the surface of the drywall. Think of it in terms of icing a cake. To spread the icing on the cake, you keep your spatula nearly flat. But to scrape the last bit out of the bowl, the blade of your spatula has to be more perpendicular to the inside surface of the bowl. If you can grasp the concept of applying and removing the compound in this manner, you're halfway home. This same approach

To cover the screws with compound, spread a generous layer over several screws in a row (top), then scrape off the excess compound, leaving a tight thin coat over the screws (above).

TIP

Punch in Holes from Missed Screws

There are always places where a screw missed the framing or was overdriven. In most of these cases a rough edge of the drywall paper is left exposed. It's nearly impossible to compound over rough paper, so give the hole a tap with the handle of your knife (see the photo below). (The metal end on the knife handle is made especially for this purpose.) Any ragged edges get pushed in below the surface so the hole can be coated cleanly.

is used with every phase, but covering the screws gives you the best practice. The angle of your knife may vary slightly with the different phases, but the concept remains the same.

Flat seams

The next phase of applying compound is working the flat seams. Recall that most of these are where two tapered factory edges meet. These (and all seams) get covered with tape that bridges the seam. Flat seams can be found on every wall and ceiling, and the process is the same for both places. Start by applying compound down the length of the seam as far as you can reach. With a little practice, you'll learn just how much to apply to make the process work well. After you've applied the compound, start at one end and push the tape into the compound. You can work directly off a roll of tape, or just get an approximate

For flat tapered-edge seams, start with a generous, even layer of compound over the seam. Work only as much area as you can reach.

length and cut off the end. When you get to the end, hold your knife tight against the drywall and tear off the excess tape.

Now go back over the seam with your knife, pressing the tape into the compound and squeezing out the excess. This process takes a lot of practice to perfect the right angle and the right amount of pressure. Too much pressure or too steep an angle and you can tear the tape or pull the tape so that it bunches up. Too little pressure and the tape doesn't adhere properly or doesn't sit perfectly flat. Always have a little compound on the knife for lubrication as well as to thoroughly impregnate the tape with compound. Work one stroke on each side of the tape to remove excess compound and finish with a stroke down the middle. The tape should be completely flat and adhered with no bubbles or dry spots, and all "ridges" of excess compound should be gone.

When you start off and first learn to tape seams, I can almost guarantee that you'll overwork the seams. When that happens, the compound begins to dry and stick to the knife, pulling off the compound instead of laying it down. Practice your strokes and angling your knife so that you use a minimum number of strokes for the desired effect.

ANOTHER WAY TO DO IT

Fiberglass Mesh Tape

Another common tape for drywall seams is fiberglass mesh. It is significantly stronger than paper tape, but it's also more expensive, and I find it harder to work with. Because of its strength and moisture resistance, I keep it on hand for very specific applications. The first is joining new drywall to existing drywall or plaster. The second is repairing drywall cracks, and the third is in areas where you've used moisture-resistant drywall, such as in a bathroom.

Start at one end and press the paper lightly into the compound so that it adheres well (top). At the end, use your knife blade as a straightedge to rip off the excess paper (above).

Inside corners

Each of these phases gets progressively more difficult. Corner seams up the ante once again. Inside corner seams occur either as ceiling-to-wall or wall-to-wall, and techniques for both are essentially the same. Coat both sides of the corner, pushing compound into any gaps. If you use short strokes to force the compound into the gap, smooth the compound before applying the tape. Paper drywall tape has a line running down the middle of the tape. Fold a length of tape lengthwise along the line, and press the tape into the compound using your knife to push the tape evenly into the corner. Now go back and smooth each side, adhering the tape and removing the excess compound. The biggest trick for me doing corners was not letting the side of my knife blade hit the adjacent side of the corner. Again, practice is the best teacher.

A word to the wise: When working inside corner seams, work all three corners (the wall-to-wall corner and the two adjacent wall-to-ceiling corners) that intersect simultaneously. When all three corners are

For inside corners, coat both sides, filling any voids between the sheets of drywall with compound (right). Fold a length of tape in half lengthwise, then press the tape into the compounded corner using the blade of the joint knife (far right).

ANOTHER WAY TO DO IT

Flat Seams without Tapered Edges

If you put the drywall up successfully, there should be only a few short flat seams without tapered edges. For these seams, start by tearing the paper off the drywall along the seam. Again, this strategy keeps you from having a raised edge on the seam that can keep the tape from lying flat. Spread the compound and tape the seam as you would ordinarily, taking extra care to make the seam as tight as possible with no taper to hide the compound.

For seams where two nontapered edges meet, tear the paper off one side to make it lie flatter when it is coated with compound and tape.

Now work each side of the corner, first squeezing out the excess compound and then smoothing the compound completely.

At the intersection between corners, lightly feather the compound back with your joint knife, so that every corner is clean and smooth at the intersection.

adhered and smooth, go back to the intersection and work outward lightly on both sides of all three corners. Keep the knife angle fairly low and the pressure very light to blend all three corners together. This detail will test the limits of your skills as well as your patience. The same principle holds true where a corner seam passes a flat seam. Your final stroke should be a light low-angle stroke outward from the corner and along the seam.

Outside corners

The last details for the first coat of compound are the outside corners. The most common treatment of outside corners starts with metal corner bead. Measure the length you need and cut the bead with tin snips. Again, precision is not required. Baseboard will cover the bottom few inches, so the bead doesn't have to run all the way to the floor. Treat the bead gingerly. It can bend easily, and once it does, it will never make a straight corner. Also, never try to use multiple pieces of bead for one corner. It is darned near impossible to

Reinforced Tape for Nonsquare Corners

Where a cathedral ceiling meets a wall, the angle is greater than 90 degrees and regular paper tape can fail in this application. For these areas, use a different kind of tape called Flex Tape®, or structural-corner system. The sides are wider and thicker for better adhesion, and the centerline of the tape is a flexible material that allows for minor movement between the ceiling and the wall. Flex Tape installs the same way as paper tape except that the runs should be done in one uninterrupted piece. And instead of tearing off the excess tape, it has to be cut with snips.

Use special structural tape for the corner between a cathedral ceiling and a wall. This tape is thicker, so you need to cut it with snips. It installs essentially the same as paper tape, but it also takes more compound on successive coats to blend it back to the drywall.

get them aligned so that they finish evenly. Once the bead is cut to length, place it over the corner and press lightly directly into the corner. The sides of the bead should flare out until they are at right angles to each other. Before you start to nail the bead, make sure there aren't any areas of the drywall that stick out more than others. These protrusions will keep the bead from pushing in evenly from top to bottom. While maintaining light pressure on the bead, push a nail into one of the holes and drive it in. Drive a nail on the opposite side to hold the bead evenly. Now move down a few feet and repeat the process. As you nail in the bead, make sure that it stays straight top to bottom. Go back and attach the bead every foot or so, making sure that it won't move around as you apply the compound.

Corner bead creates a substantial gap that has to be filled to blend the corner back into the plane of the drywall. A 6-in. joint knife won't give you a wide enough swath of compound. Instead, use a 10-in. taping knife. Start by loading the bead with compound. Push compound into the bead so that it keys into the holes, using strokes perpendicular to the bead. Use the corner to gently scrape the compound off the knife. When you've loaded the corner on both sides, add compound to your taping knife and run a smooth stroke along the bead, letting the knife blade ride on the corner. Now go back and remove the excess compound, this time with one side of the taping knife riding on the bead and the other side on the drywall. After working both sides, you'll notice chunks of compound building up on the corner. Carefully push the edge of the knife blade up the outside of the bead to remove this residue. This step is another that demands precise control of the angle as well as pressure on the knife. Where the outside corner meets the ceiling or another seam, let the knife strokes flare away from the outside corner. When you've mastered that technique, you can collect your drywall diploma!

To attach outside corner bead, press the bead directly toward the corner and nail it on both sides. Make sure it is perfectly straight and continue down the bead, pressing and nailing it into place.

As with the other seams, first scrape off the excess compound, letting the taping knife ride on the corner bead, then go back over the area to smooth and feather the compound back to the surface of the drywall.

For the second coat of compound over the screws, use the same technique as before, applying a generous layer of compound and then scraping it off tight to the drywall.

To apply a second coat of compound to the flat seams, smooth on the compound with a 10-in. taping knife that extends the coat a few inches on either side of the first coat.

Second Coat of Compound

By comparison with the first coat of compound, the second coat is easy, especially if you're getting the hang of knife angle and pressure. Before you fill your mudpan, go back over your work on the first coat. You can easily scrape off slight ridges with a dry joint knife used like a chisel. If you must, lightly sand with sanding screen on a block or pad. Sandpaper works in a pinch, but sanding screen lets the dust pass through the screen without clogging it up. You should be able to get away with using 120-grit (fine) screen. Resist the temptation to hold the screen in your hand. It is very difficult to apply flat pressure with just your hand. Sanding pads on poles even let you sand ceilings without the use of staging.

All the tough work of taping and filling was done on the first coat. The second coat of compound adds another wider layer, feathering the compound out further to the surface of the drywall. We used the joint knife for most of the first coat (except for the outside corners). Now our tool of choice will be a 10-in. taping knife. But keep your joint knife handy—you'll need it for the second coat on the screws as well as for the inside corners. For the screws, use the same motions as with the first coat: Slather on and scrape off. The second layer should be slightly wider than the first layer.

For flat seams, add the second coat of compound with the taping knife. Coat a section of the seam with a thin, even layer, then scrape the layer tight so that it extends a few inches on either side of the first layer. At this point, the entire tapered area should be filled flush with the surface of the drywall. One detail of flat seams that can be a pain on the second coat is electrical boxes that fall on the seam. The taping coat just went on either side of the box, but to fill the seam taper completely you need to go over the box. Inevitably some compound ends up in the box. I've seen some overexuberant drywallers fill boxes completely. The compound comes out pretty quickly after the fact, but with a little finesse, you can minimize the amount of compound in the electrical boxes.

Inside corners are treated a little differently on the second coat. You do only one side at a time. This plan of attack ensures that you don't mess up the compound on the adjacent wall. The joint knife works fine for this step because it's smaller and easier to control. The blade is plenty wide enough to feather the compound onto the surface of the drywall. Coat all of the corners that intersect on this coat. On the final coat, you coat the other side of each of the corners. If you did your outside corners well the first time, you should only need to do a final coat on them. But go back over them and fill any low spots you might find.

Final Coat of Compound

Again, if you were careful applying the second coat, sanding should not be necessary. Go back over every seam and make sure there are no ridges left from the edge of the knife. If you find any, remove them by pushing your knife blade over the surface like a wide chisel. Sand lightly if you need to, but don't forget to use the sanding screen and pad, and use a finer grit screen this time around, 220 grit if you can find it.

This coat should be your last, so make it look as smooth and as even as you can get it. For covering the screw holes on the final coat, switch to the 10-in. taping knife, using the same technique as before only in a slightly wider pass (see the top photo on p. 66).

On inside corners, work the opposite side of each corner from the second coat. Use the 6-in. joint knife for this step for maximum control. Apply the compound as before, spreading a thin, even layer and then scraping it off. But on the final pass, change your grip on the knife and apply very light pressure to smooth and feather the coat. Using the same grip, feather the

Where an electrical box interrupts a seam, let the taping knife ride over the box. Any compound that gets in the box is easily removed when it hardens.

Inside corners get only two coats of compound. But coat only one side at a time on this coat to avoid messing up the compound on the adjacent side.

For the final coat of compound over the screws, switch to a 10-in. taping knife for wider coverage.

compound outward from the intersection of the corners in each direction.

For outside corners, apply the final coat with a 12-in. taping knife, extending the layer of compound beyond the layers below. The surface should be a fair, even line from the corner bead to the bare drywall. If you find any noticeable hollows, fill them and feather them into the rest of the applied compound.

The final coat on the flat seams is particularly challenging. Of all the places on the walls and ceilings, they are the most glaring when not finished properly. Instead of just going over the middle of the seam as you've done up to this point, spread compound in a thin layer on both sides of the seam using a 12-in. taping knife. Your final coat will then be 20 in. to 24 in. wide, but the finished seam will be invisible when painted. I watched Alain as he worked the seam. After spreading the compound, he made three successive passes. On each pass the angle of the knife became

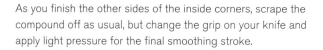

As you finish the other sides of the inside corners, scrape the compound off as usual, but change the grip on your knife and apply light pressure for the final smoothing stroke.

Outside corners should also need only two coats of compound. Use a 12-in. taping knife to apply a wide final layer of compound.

flatter and the pressure on the knife got lighter. The final pass was barely touching the surface.

Drywall wrap-up

When the compounding is finished, check the surfaces with a work light to make sure there are no places that need filling or sanding. Some people I've worked with insist that a light sanding of the final coat is necessary, but the jury is still out on that one. If this is one of your first major drywall jobs, sanding might be required to make all the surfaces appear as one. Again, use a fine sanding screen on a pad, sanding in light strokes. Don't overdo the sanding. It's not hard to raise the grain on the drywall paper, and once you do, a super-thin layer of compound is the only way to cover it up properly.

The company that Alain works for, Barber Drywall, includes priming the walls as part of their package. Once you're satisfied with the drywall job, it's not a bad idea to take the opportunity to prime the drywall with a good-quality primer. I'd also add a finish coat of paint, especially on the ceilings. We'll talk more about painting later on.

ESSENTIAL TECHNIQUE

Testing for Flatness

As you apply the final coats of compound, be aware of places that might need to be filled to make them flat. Your knife will behave differently as it passes over these spots. When you feel a difference, check the spot by using the edge of your knife as a straightedge (see the photo below). Then go back and add more compound to that area, feathering it out further in every direction.

As you apply the final layer of compound to outside corners and flat seams, be conscious of low areas that need to be filled. Gauge the voids using the edge of your taping knife.

Work both sides of a flat seam in three steps. At each step the angle of the knife gets progressively lower and the pressure on the blade gets progressively lighter. The first step is scraping off the excess compound. The next step smoothes the compound even more. The final step feathers the compound to the surface of the drywall.

Floors

Most contractors I know proceed to the floor installation after the drywall. I can already hear the head scratching, and those looks of puzzlement are completely understandable. You are going to be putting a finish material directly where it's going to receive the most damage—under foot! Although that fact is inescapable, many factors support the decision. Think of the flooring as the first "finish material" that is installed. It completes the floors of the house. Now realize that for a finished look, it's much easier to create attractive joints between materials when you apply those materials on top of the flooring instead of running the flooring to the finish materials. Those finish materials include baseboard, doors, and door trim, as well as the cabinetry.

There are many different types of flooring, from various types of wood, to resilient flooring (vinyl, linoleum, and cork), to tile (ceramic and stone), and don't forget carpeting. With some of those types of flooring, installation should be left to the pros, or at least to someone with extensive installation experience. This chapter deals with the very basic installation of wood flooring, one of the most common flooring choices, and tile, which is a good choice for areas that get exposed to excessive moisture, such as bathrooms and kitchens. With both of these choices, a simple installation is, well, simple. However, both wood and tile flooring can get pretty complicated once you start adding borders, inlays, and other decorative touches.

Wood Flooring

Wood flooring has been around almost as long as houses themselves. Wood gives you an attractive, durable, and easy-to-maintain flooring surface. In addition to a wide variety of species available, you can purchase wood flooring as interlocking strips or as planks in widths up to 2 ft. if you're willing to pay the price. Plus, wood flooring is available unfinished or with a factory finish. It is also available as solid wood or as a laminated veneer product, which is essentially plywood with the top veneer made of whatever species you want. The flooring for this installation is 3¼-in.-wide unfinished red oak strips. This flooring is the most popular choice in most areas in the country. Do your homework and figure out which product is best for your situation and budget.

If putting the floor down at this stage of construction still makes you uneasy, please realize that most of the floor does not get sanded and finished at this point. The unfinished wood is still technically a "finish" product, but it gets sanded and finished at a later stage in the building process. That said, even unfinished flooring needs to be protected from the rigors of finishing the house. A piece of equipment dropped on or dragged across the floor can inflict permanent damage to the flooring that no amount of sanding or finishing can disguise.

SHOULD I TACKLE THIS MYSELF?

Pros

Installing wood-strip flooring is pretty easy and straight-forward for a person with moderate carpentry experience. The strips usually lock together with tongue-and-groove joints on the edges and ends. It's a good job for someone planning to work either alone or with others. Most tool rental centers carry pneumatic flooring nailers, which are the best way to install the wood strips in most cases. Installing your own flooring can also save you a bundle of money. Most professional installers charge many dollars per square foot for installation on top of the price of materials.

Cons

If you are a person who can't stand repetitive, tedious work, maybe installing wood floors isn't for you. Numerous nails have to be driven into each strip, and that monotonous action can get old, even for a seasoned installer. Installing strip flooring requires swinging a mallet in a hunched-over position—a sure recipe for a sore back. And like most of the other finishing steps, a professional flooring installer will get the job done much more quickly and efficiently than you can by yourself.

TOOLS NEEDED

- Pneumatic flooring nailer
- Flooring mallet
- Pneumatic brad nailer
- Compressor
- Miter saw
- Router

A floor nailer and mallet are indispensable tools for installing a wood floor. The mallet strikes the ram on the nailer, which in turn drives the nail. This nailer is a pneumatic version.

The first step in estimating for wood floors is to determine what rooms will receive the flooring. Wood flooring is adversely affected by moisture, so it is probably not the wisest choice for damp places such as bathrooms or a laundry, although some folks still choose wood for these areas. Measure the area of each room that gets the flooring and as a rule of thumb, add 10 percent for waste. Then divide your total square footage by the square footage in each bundle. Typically that number is around 20 sq. ft. Shop around, though, because there are always bargains out there on flooring. But beware of cheaper, more rustic grades of flooring. Those grades can generate a lot more waste, and your estimate needs to be adjusted accordingly.

Before the installation

Wood flooring is an organic material, and as such it can move dramatically as it absorbs or gives up moisture. Houses under construction are notorious for having moist environments, especially right after drywall installation. If your house is in a cooler climate and you are installing the wood floors in the heating season, you should bring the house up to temperature to dry out the interior before the wood flooring is delivered. In warmer climates, the air conditioning might have to be turned on to cool and dry the interior. In either scenario, that process could take a few days, so schedule accordingly. It obviously helps to have the home's heater or air conditioning functional at this stage.

The wood flooring is delivered to the house having acclimated to the temperature and humidity in the storage facility. Before you begin installing the flooring, it needs to acclimate to the temperature and humidity inside the house. If you install the flooring too soon, it will continue to acclimate after it's installed. If it continues to dry out after it's installed, gaps can form between the strips. If the flooring gains moisture after it's installed, it can buckle. When properly acclimated, the flooring moves in concert with the rest of the house with minimal problems.

Load the flooring into the house

Ideally you should bring the wood flooring into the house a week or so before you start to install it, but even just a few days makes a difference in helping the wood adapt to the environment inside the house. Stack bundles of flooring in each room. Note the direction of the installation and stack the bundles near the last area that is to be covered. If not, you'll end up handling the bundles a second time.

Monitor the Humidity with a Thermo-Hygrometer

To determine if the house is at the right temperature and relative humidity, invest in a digital thermometer/hygrometer (humidity reader). Keep it on hand all through the finishing stages of your home. Inexpensive models are available for under $20. Ideally the humidity in the house should be down in the low 30s, and the temperature should be at least in the 60s. If you paid attention in science class, you know that as air increases in temperature, it can hold more humidity. So don't let the house get too warm or you might have trouble getting the humidity down.

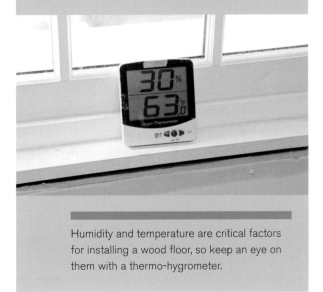

Humidity and temperature are critical factors for installing a wood floor, so keep an eye on them with a thermo-hygrometer.

Stack bundles of flooring in the rooms so that they can acclimate to the environment in the house over a few days. Note that this material should have been stacked next to the window wall and will have to be moved before the flooring can be installed.

Paper or no paper?

As a contractor, I always put down either red rosin paper or 15-lb. felt (tar paper) over the subfloor before installing a wood floor, but never quite understood why. While at *Fine Homebuilding* I asked many professional carpenters and flooring installers why. Generally they'd sort of hem and haw, mumble a little bit, and then change the subject to the Red Sox or something else. It's still hard to nail down a definitive reason for using paper under wood flooring, but it most likely is a holdover from a bygone building era.

When I asked the pros whom I photographed for this chapter, the answer was twofold. The first reason is that the paper acts as a moisture barrier between the flooring and a damp area below, such as a basement or crawlspace. But in this day and age of oriented-strand-board (OSB) sheathing, where the tongue-and-groove joints between the sheets are glued as the sheets go down, moisture is probably not the issue it once was in most cases. We have developed ways of sealing and detailing crawlspaces to minimize moisture, and insulating basement walls can go a long way toward keeping basements dry. And if the paper is supposed to be a moisture barrier, why use it under flooring on upper floors? If you do have a situation where the space under your floor is excessively damp, it might be

better to choose a type of flooring that is not as affected by moisture as wood.

The second reason given is that paper helps to stop floor squeaks. Again, this theory is a myth. Floor squeaks are most often caused by the subfloor rubbing against a joist, or from a nail that moves up and down as the floor flexes. Paper does not stop that kind of movement and therefore does not stop floor squeaks.

For me, the paper serves a third, more selfish purpose. It gives you a clean, fresh surface to work from. Consider that so far the floor sheathing has endured the framing, the rough-in of the utilities, insulation, and then the drywall, all of which have

Material Choice: Tar Paper or Red Rosin Paper?

Both of these materials work fine under wood floors, so which one should you use? As a card-carrying cheapskate, the first factor in choosing for me is cost. Check with your building supply company to see which is more expensive. The second is the fact that tar paper or felt paper is impregnated with asphalt, so using it indoors can introduce toxins associated with asphalt. If you happen to be one of those folks who is environmentally sensitive, I'd opt for the more innocuous red rosin paper.

Before you start to install the flooring, sweep the floor thoroughly to remove any construction dust and debris. Be sure to scrape off any lumps of joint compound and sink any nail heads that might be sticking up.

added debris to the floor—from sawdust to stripped-off wire insulation to bits of gypsum and globs of joint compound. Part of the prep work is sweeping the floor, but it's nearly impossible to get the floor perfectly clean and free of debris. The paper gives you a clean slate—or in this case, clean substrate to work from.

Putting down the paper

Before you put down the paper, give the floor a good sweeping. Use a stiff broom and sweep vigorously to remove as much debris as possible. Lay down the paper in the same direction the flooring will run, and start from the same point as where the flooring will start. If it is a large central room such as a living room or den, you would typically begin along one of the longest walls. If the room opens off a hallway, begin at the door and work your way to the opposite wall.

Start at one wall and roll out the paper to the opposite wall. Lift the roll slightly, and with a utility knife, slice along the joint between the floor and the wall. I've seen some guys paper the whole floor at once and then lay out the flooring, but I like to roll out lengths as I need to.

Construction paper, either felt or red rosin, gives you a clean, fresh surface to work from.

Racking the floor is laying out the material in roughly the same pattern as it will be installed. Instead of cutting pieces to length, just set a slightly longer piece on top of the piece before. The installer will cut the end pieces to the proper length.

Racking

Racking is laying out the flooring beforehand, roughly, as it will be installed. If you're working alone, you may opt to spread out the material as you go. You'll always need to do some adjustment of the courses while nailing, but the process goes more quickly after you've racked the floor.

Set a bundle of strips on the floor and cut the straps. (You need to sort through the bundle as you search for specific lengths, and that process works better if you open the bundle on the floor.) The lengths in the bundle are random, so grab the first couple layers and start laying the strips on the floor, again starting from where you plan to begin the installation. Make sure the tongue edges of the strips face in the direction of the installation.

At this point don't try to be precise with the length—that step happens during the actual installation. In fact, don't try to cut any lengths at this stage. Work your way from one end and spread the pieces across, close together, but not necessarily interlocking for now. When you get to the other end, find a piece that is a couple of inches long and leave the piece stacked over its neighbor.

Staggering butt seams

As you work your way across the floor, the goal is to lay out the successive courses so that the butt seams of the boards don't line up closely within two courses. Many installers try to keep close seams three courses apart. The job then becomes a big jigsaw puzzle. Obviously, completing one course at a time all the way across the room would not be an efficient use of time and effort, so try to work four or five courses at once. Start by stacking up lengths that are 8 in. to 12 in. shorter than the piece below. Use those pieces as the starters for successive courses. They should line up like stair steps, with the ends already properly staggered. Add random lengths to each course, working all five

Staggered Seams: Good and Bad

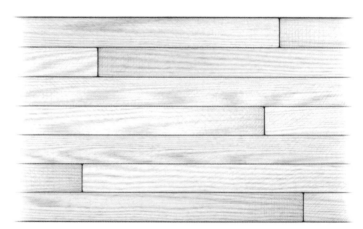

Good: Closely spaced seams two courses apart; seams on adjacent courses at least 10 in. apart

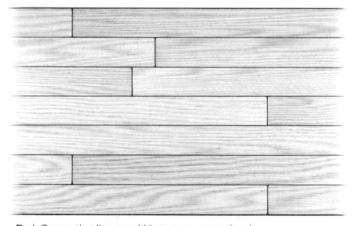

Bad: Seams that line up within two courses; closely spaced seams on adjacent courses

courses across the room at once. Just be mindful of the butt seams in the preceding courses as you lay the pieces down. And realize that you can combine a couple of shorter pieces to make up the length that you need.

I recommend working through most of each bundle before opening a new one. This strategy uses up the shorter lengths as you progress across the floor, and those short pieces get distributed evenly throughout the floor. Otherwise you get stuck having to use a pile of shorties at one end of the floor, and all the seams will make that area look more "busy" than the rest. As the flooring nears the edge of the paper, roll out another course of paper and continue racking. Realize that the racking process does not dictate strict placement of the pieces. Adjustments always have to be made during installation. What racking does is to give the installer predistributed courses that can be nailed in quickly and efficiently. Also, racking does not cover the entire floor. There are gaps between the racked courses that come out during installation, meaning that the installer always has to lay out the last few courses.

Install the flooring

With the paper down and the flooring distributed throughout the room, you are ready to begin nailing the flooring into place. Round up the tools you'll need, including the flooring nailer, flooring mallet, and pneumatic brad nailer and finish nailer. Pick up the first couple of racked courses to clear the space you need to begin nailing.

To make the process go more quickly, make a stack of lengths successively shorter as starter pieces (top), then set them out like stair steps to begin successive courses (above).

Wear Sneakers

When installing unfinished flooring, wear sneakers or shoes with non-marking soles. Many work shoes have soles that can leave black marks on the floor. Any marks will just have to be sanded out later. Plus, sneakers will let your feet slide the boards into position.

Thresholds

The beginning courses of flooring have to be solidly anchored so they remain stationary as the rest of the flooring is nailed in. If your installation begins at a wall with a doorway, solid backing needs to be provided across the rough opening of the door. If the flooring on the other side of the doorway is already installed, go ahead and install the threshold pieces. If the flooring is not installed on the other side of the doorway, or if the doorway is to receive a different kind of threshold (such as a marble threshold for a bathroom), a temporary block is needed to give the first course of flooring solid backing. The temporary block is snugged against the back of the first course in the doorway and either screwed or nailed into place. A similar block or strip should also be used at the top of a stairway.

Where a threshold is perpendicular to the flooring courses, run the courses of flooring until they intersect with the doorway. The groove end of the butt should land at the threshold. The first threshold piece is then cut and set into place with its tongue locking into the butt groove of the course. Place a framing square between the flooring course and the threshold (see the top left photo on p. 76). When they are perfectly square to each other, face-nail the threshold and the flooring course to hold them both in place. The rest of the courses can then begin at the threshold with factory-cut butts.

Where a different material will be used for the threshold (such as in this doorway into a bathroom), nail or screw a temporary block to back up the first course of flooring.

When the stairs are finished, a nosing will butt into the flooring. Until then, a temporary strip holds the flooring tight.

The first course needs to be anchored and backed up properly. Drive finish nails through the faces of the boards in that course as well as angled through the tongues. In the doorway, complete the threshold to the flooring on the other side.

That strategy leaves you a groove facing into the adjacent room instead of a tongue. So glue a spline into the other side of the threshold to intersect the flooring in that room. Splines are narrow strips of wood sold by the flooring companies sized specifically to slip into the flooring groove and stick out the same distance as the tongue. Splines allow you to reverse the direction of the tongue and groove, and also to create a place for the nailer to sit on to ensure proper nailing.

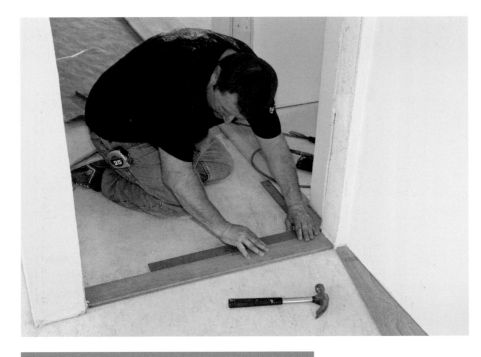

Where a threshold is at right angles to the flooring direction, run the first course of flooring that intersects with the threshold, and then square the threshold to that course.

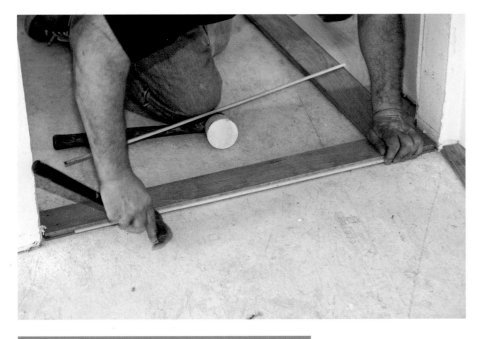

To reverse the direction of the flooring, glue and nail a factory-made spline into the groove of the flooring. The reversed edge can then be nailed with a flooring nailer.

The rest of the courses can start at the threshold using the factory butt cuts.

Expansion gaps

We've already discussed how dynamic wood flooring can be. It had to be acclimated to the house's environment to minimize its movement due to changes in humidity levels. But that's not the end of it. Even nailed securely to the floor sheathing, wood flooring expands as humidity increases. Wood expands across its width but not its length. So a gap should be left between the edge of the first course and the wall to allow the flooring to expand. Most flooring installers recommend the gap to be at least $\frac{3}{8}$ in. By the way, by installing the flooring first, the baseboard will cover the gap easily.

The first course of flooring guides the rest of the floor, so that course has to be absolutely straight. A snapped chalkline is the best way to guide that first

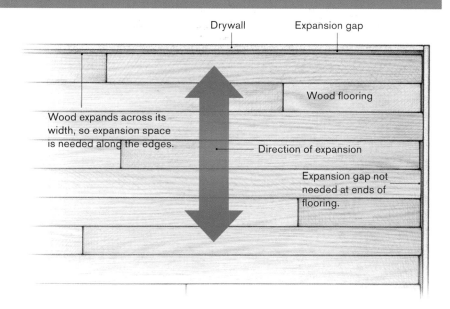

Wood Floor Expansion

Drywall   Expansion gap

Wood flooring

Wood expands across its width, so expansion space is needed along the edges.

Direction of expansion

Expansion gap not needed at ends of flooring.

Leave $\frac{1}{4}$-in. to $\frac{3}{8}$-in. space along the edge of the flooring to allow room for the flooring to expand and contract freely.

TIP

Mark Joists before Face Nailing

To secure the first and last courses, finish nails should be driven through the face of the flooring, through the floor sheathing, and into the floor joists. Floor joists are easy to find in the bare floor sheathing (just look for the nail heads). Mark their location on the wall just above the level of the flooring.

Before you cover up the subfloor, mark the joist locations on the wall just above the height of the floor. These marks will guide the face nails that are driven into the final courses.

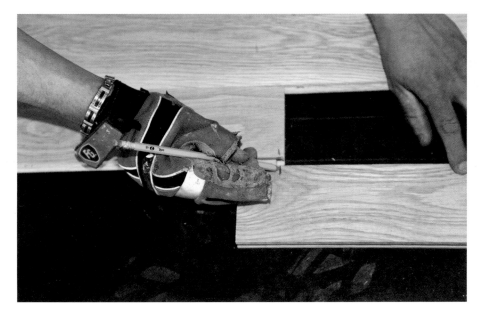

Instead of measuring the length of an end piece, reverse its direction and mark the length from the piece before. Leave a little extra room for the piece to slip in easily; baseboard will cover any minor gap along the wall.

course, especially with long walls. Any variation in straightness becomes compounded as you work across the floor. With the first course aligned to the snapped line, face-nail it with 2½-in. finish nails along the wall. In addition, drive the same type of nails diagonally just above the tongue. When the first course is secured, you can install the rest of the courses.

Work multiple courses at one time

With your sneaker, pull the pieces from the "rack" in front of you. Instead of working one course all the way across the room, work one area. Usually this area is about 5 ft. or 6 ft. wide, so nail in the pieces of the first course to about that length. Pull over the next course and nail in the pieces as far as you can without overlapping the end of a previous course. The result is the same stepped arrangement we had during the racking process. When you've nailed in as many courses as you can without overlapping (usually four or five), move over and add the next pieces to build the "steps" again. Continue this process until you reach the opposite wall. Recall that as we racked the floor, we left the last piece on the courses slightly long. When you get to the opposite wall, measure and cut as many end pieces as you can carry in one trip to the saw. Cut the end pieces so that they slip in easily—the baseboard will hide any minor gaps at the ends of the courses, so ⅛ in. to ¼ in. short is fine.

Instead of measuring to mark the length of the final piece in the course, reverse its direction and let it extend past the piece before, which is already nailed in. On the piece before, make a mark about ⅛ in. from the bottom of the groove, or ⅛ in. from the end of the tongue, whichever is exposed. Transfer that mark to the reversed end piece. With the piece reversed, the mark is already on the end you're cutting off. Cut to the line with a chopsaw or miter saw, and the end piece should slip easily into place.

As you work your way across the room, develop a rhythm. Professional installers use their feet to slip the next piece into place. A tap on the end of the board locks the butt in place. Then the board is nailed every 6 in. to 8 in., starting a couple of inches from each end. The action is repeated continuously as you work across the floor, pulling the boards from the racked sections, tapping them into position, and nailing them in. As you put the boards in, keep an eye on the butt seams to make sure they don't line up too closely.

Flooring nailers are ingenious and very specialized tools. The foot of the nailer steps over the edge of the board, aligning the nail precisely with the top of the tongue at an angle of about 45 degrees. All nailers are activated by striking a spring-loaded ram with a flooring mallet that has a rubber face on one side and a metal face on the other. With older manual nailers, the ram sits on top of the nail. Striking the ram physically forces the nail into the wood. With newer pneumatic flooring nailers, striking the ram activates a pneumatic piston that drives the nail. These newer nailers take a lot less force and put a lot less wear and tear on the guy with the mallet. The beauty of the flooring nailer is that the action of striking the ram at an angle snugs the edge of the board against its neighbor. The result is a tight floor with no gaps between the boards. As a word of caution, I've seen flooring nailers close gaps of a strong 1/16 in. They are not meant to close gaps that are the width of the tongue. As you move the boards into place, tap them along the tongue until they mate closely with the neighboring board. If the boards are reluctant to slide together, check for a damaged tongue or debris in the groove. Do not try to force the boards together.

Scribe around obstacles

Every time a flooring course encounters an obstacle or interruption, such as a doorway to a closet, the pieces need to be cut to fit around that obstacle. The good news is that at this stage a tight precise fit is not necessary, with the baseboard and door trim coming along later to hide the fit. In fact, be sure to maintain the expansion gap even if the edge only runs a few inches along a wall.

The best way to scribe around an obstacle is first to nail in the pieces over to the one you need to cut. Set the next piece in place extending past the obstacle. Slide the butt seams together, keeping the back edge parallel with the installed flooring and leaving the expansion gap at the back edge of the board. Mark either side of the obstacle on the board, leaving 1/4 in. or so of play. (By the way, always avoid a butt seam landing in the middle of the obstacle. You'll have a much easier time keeping the course straight if the piece wraps around and continues on a bit.) Next, square the marks across the board. Measure the distance that the board has to move over to align with the course. Mark that measurement from the back

Develop an installation rhythm as you work across the floor. First pull the board into position with your foot (top), then tap the end with a mallet to close the butt seam (middle), and nail the board every 6 in. to 8 in. (above).

ESSENTIAL TECHNIQUE

Making an End-Matched Butt Joint

As you run flooring through most of an entire house, or even through a whole room, you'll need to use cutoff pieces that don't have grooves in the butt ends for end matching. Cutting those grooves is easy with the proper tools. And being able to create the end-matched joint means using up a lot of material that would otherwise go to waste.

First cut the end perfectly square on your chopsaw. Next, put a slotting cutter bit in a router (a router mounted in a router table is fine if you're more comfortable with that arrangement). A slotting cutter is a bit that you "build." It has an arbor with a shank at one end that goes into the router. The other end of the arbor has a threaded shaft where you mount the cutter and bearing. (Arbors come in various shaft sizes to fit whatever router you're using. As someone who has had the scary and dangerous experience of an undersize router-bit shaft failing, I recommend using a minimum 1/2-in. shank router and bit for a slotting cutter.)

The cutter itself is flat and slips over the threaded shaft. Slotting cutters come in various cutting widths. Choose a width to match the size of the groove you want to cut, in this case 1/4 in. Next, a bearing slips over the shaft. The bearing sets the depth of the cut by riding on the material and stopping the bit from cutting deeper. Bearings come in various diameters—the smaller the diameter, the deeper the cut. Use a bearing that allows you to match the depth of the factory grooves in the boards. Finally, a washer and nut go on to secure the cutter and bearing on the shaft. I always use a locking nut for this task to make sure it stays put. Now move the base of the router up or down to position the cutter to match the flooring perfectly. A scrap of flooring works as a gauge to make sure the cutter is positioned properly.

After you've made the square cut on the end of the board, place the board securely on a flat surface. If you're used to handling a router, you can hold the board with one hand and operate the router with the other. A better and safer option is to clamp the board to the table and keep both hands on the router. Always move the router in a direction opposite to the rotation of the blade. (Most routers have an arrow to eliminate any confusion about rotation direction.) With the router running, ease the cutter into one side of the butt, and then move slowly and carefully across the end, maintaining the pressure of the router against the flooring.

To make a grooved butt seam, first cut the end of the piece at 90 degrees (top). Then use a slotting cutter in a router: The cutting blade makes the slot and the bearing controls the depth (middle). Move the router carefully across the end of the board in the opposite direction from the router rotation (above).

edge of the board on each of your squared lines. Using a straightedge, draw a line across to connect the marks (a length of flooring makes a good straightedge). Cut out the area you just marked. There are many options, but a jigsaw is probably your safest bet. When the outlined material is removed, put the piece in position to continue the course around the obstacle. At this point, just drive a couple of nails to secure the butt end in place. Don't assume that both sides of a wide closet opening will be in line with your flooring course. Instead, stretch a chalkline across the room, lining it up with the pieces you've already nailed in. Two people make this step go more smoothly: one gauging the line along the edge of the course while the other moves the line side to side (see the top photo on p. 82). (Note that

To scribe a cut around an obstacle, first butt the end of the piece to be cut against its neighbor, keeping the edge parallel to the course before. Mark both sides of the cut (top), then square the marks down (right). Measure the distance to the previous course and then mark that distance on both sides of the cut (below). Connect the marks with a straight line and make your cut.

Set up a chalkline along the course and adjust it until the course is straight.

it may be necessary to remove a small area of paper to snap the line.) Cut the next piece that butts into your scribed piece, and set it in place along the chalkline. As a final check, sight down the edge of the boards to make sure they form a perfectly straight line. Face-nail the boards to anchor them securely. (For all intents and purposes, these boards actually form a starter course.) And don't forget to nail off the rest of that course across the scribed piece. The next course can now go in, again making sure to leave the expansion gap if necessary. Complete the next course all the way across the room to reinforce the flooring before resuming the multiple-course process. Using the pattern from the racking process, work five or six courses at once in a step pattern.

Set the next piece in place and eyeball the line to make sure it's perfectly straight (above). Then secure the piece with finish nails through the faces of the boards as well as angled through the tongues of the boards (left).

Different nailing for the final courses

When you reach the opposite wall from where you started, you'll soon realize that you're running out of mallet-swinging room. Realistically, the last three full courses should be nailed using a different strategy if you're installing 3¼-in.-wide strips (five or six courses if you're installing the 2¼-in. strips). First mark the joist locations on the wall above the flooring level. Instead of looking for the nail heads as before, you can find one and measure 16 in. on center for the rest.

The first two of the last courses can be nailed in with a finish nailer. Just as you did with the starting course, fire the nails into the boards diagonally through the top of the tongue. Working with the finish gun doesn't give you the benefit of driving the courses together, so you need to pry them into place as you nail. One way to pry the boards over is with a large flat screwdriver. With the blade of the screwdriver against the tongue, tap the handle until the tip of the blade digs into the floor sheathing slightly. Now pull back on

Run the entire next course across the room (above), making sure to maintain expansion room between any edge that runs along a wall (below).

The last few courses cannot be nailed with the floor nailer, so use a finish nailer through the tongues of the boards (above).

Expansion gap

For areas that need force to keep gaps between the strips closed, pry against the strip with a large screwdriver as you nail.

the screwdriver to hold the boards together while you drive the nails. If the last full course is close to the wall, use a flat bar to snug the board against its neighbor. Tapping on the board with a hammer or the mallet while prying can help the boards nest together properly. With no room to fire nails into the tongue, the final full course should be face-nailed.

If you're lucky, the last course goes into place perfectly with the proper expansion gap. If you're really lucky, the last course is also perfectly parallel. But Murphy's Law notwithstanding, neither of these conditions usually exists. To fill in the last partial-width course, you'll need to rip the flooring to the proper width. First lay out the full course and cut the last piece to length. Now go along and measure the space that needs to be filled, remembering to subtract $3/8$ in. for expansion. If the course is not parallel with the wall, the gap will grow from one end to another. Because the edge will be covered with baseboard, just rip each board to the smaller size of the gap. There is no need to make a tapered rip. If, for instance, the gap goes from $5/8$ in. to $3/4$ in. over the length of a board, rip that board to $5/8$ in. Go along the course, number the boards, and mark the size of the rip on each one. Remember to leave space for expansion.

If the boards are reluctant to seat together, tap them lightly with the rubber side of the mallet while you apply pressure with a flat bar.

The best tool for ripping is a tablesaw. If the strips are narrow, make sure you use a push stick to finish your cut. When you've cut all the pieces to their designated width, spread glue along the tongue of the last installed board. Use a flat bar to get the edges mated properly and face-nail the strip. Face nails can ruin a sanding disc or belt, so after nailing off the last courses, be sure to go back and set all the face nails.

Now you can go back and complete any other flooring in the room, such as in a closet. Recall that we face-nailed the first course that went across the threshold (the scribed piece was part of the threshold). That left the groove edge of the flooring facing into closet. So as before, glue a spline into the groove to reverse the flooring direction. With the spline in place,

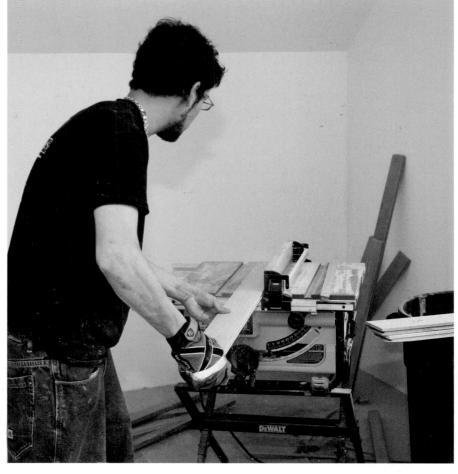

Rip the strips to width on a tablesaw.

Spread carpenter's glue along the tongue of the last full course (above left), then pry and face nail the filler strip into position (above right).

you can nail across the opening with the flooring nailer. The rest of the flooring in the closet can then be completed like a miniature version of the room.

A little prefinish goes a long way

Ordinarily, I would now say, "Let the finish carpentry begin!" When all the finish work is done, the flooring crew comes back for sanding and finishing. That's the way I always did it. But the flooring crew I photographed had a smarter idea. Sanding floors along walls and in confined areas like closets without damaging the baseboard is difficult and labor intensive. If the closet storage systems are any more than a pole and a shelf, sanding around them is a pain. The same goes for sanding around cabinets if the wood floor extends into the kitchen.

This crew sanded every closet, along with the entire kitchen area. Bigger walk-in closets were done with a large professional floor sander. Smaller closets were done with random orbital sanders with 60-grit discs. The long edges of the flooring are usually pretty even, but the ends can be notoriously wavy. So the

At the closet, reverse the direction of the flooring with a spline (above) and then nail the course with the floor nailer from that side (right). The rest of the closet can be completed like a miniature version of the room.

crew sanded along the walls in every room where the ends of the flooring hit to make it easier to install the baseboard later. After sanding, they thoroughly vacuumed and then applied a coat of sealer on those areas. After 24 hours they came back, lightly sanded, vacuumed again, and put down a base coat of varnish.

Before the finish work begins, certain floor areas of the house are sanded and prefinished. These areas include the kitchen, where cabinets will sit, and closets with complex storage systems (right). In addition, sand the ends of the boards along the wall to make baseboard installation easier (below left).

Vacuum the floor thoroughly and then apply a coat of sealer (left). After the sealer dries, the sealed areas are lightly sanded and given a first coat of varnish.

Sanding and Finishing

When my Rhode Island raised ranch was about 10 years old, I tore out the carpet and installed beautiful southern yellow pine in 10-in.-wide boards. I painstakingly drove screws into countersunk holes that I filled with mahogany plugs with the grain all oriented in the same direction, just like they'd taught me at the boat shop. The floor was gorgeous. The only thing left was the sanding and finishing.

That's where I made my mistake. I went down to the tool rental place and got a professional drum sander along with an edge sander. I got home and dug into the sanding—literally. It was a battle that I lost miserably, as I tried to get a smooth surface on the floor. My friend Rob summed it up when he came to visit. As he climbed the stairs and the floor was in plane with his line of sight he asked, "Did you sand this with a bulldozer?" From then on I always installed the floors, but would leave the floor sanding to the pros. If you've never handled a professional sander before, I'd consider swallowing your pride and letting a professional do your sanding and finishing. You and your floor will be glad you did.

Tiling a Floor

Wood floors are great for most areas, but as we've already discussed, they can be problematic in high-moisture areas such as bathrooms and kitchens. I've seen wood used in many kitchens and bathrooms, but usually after a few years the water takes its toll on areas that receive frequent soakings: around sinks, outside shower doors, and next to toilets. Moisture always seems to find a way to get under the finish, and then begins its task of discoloring and destroying the wood. Refinishing is always labor intensive and rarely re-creates the floor that you had when it was new.

The trouble is that wood is an organic substance and as such it breaks down when exposed to moisture. A better plan is to choose a nonorganic material that is naturally resistant to moisture intrusion, such as stone or tile. When installed properly, tile floors are

Tile is a good choice of materials for areas prone to high moisture such as bathrooms and kitchens.

Tile Underlayment

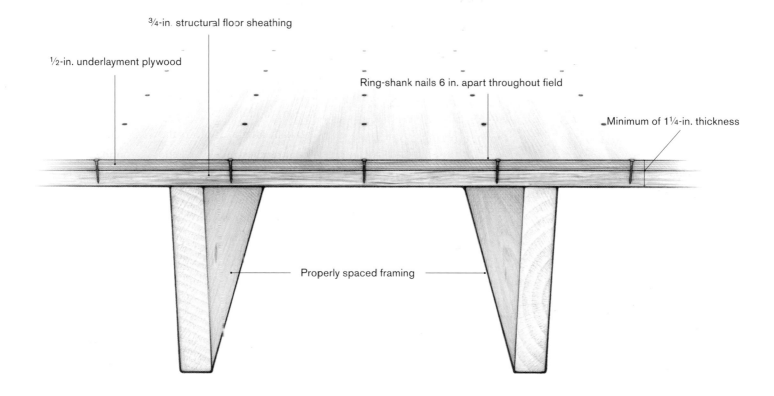

¾-in. structural floor sheathing

½-in. underlayment plywood

Ring-shank nails 6 in. apart throughout field

Minimum of 1¼-in. thickness

Properly spaced framing

long-lasting and wear-resistant. And because they are nonorganic, tile and stone won't rot when exposed to moisture over time.

It's important to have a proper substrate under every tiled floor to keep the floor from flexing, which can cause the tile to crack. The most basic minimum substrate is 1¼ in. of plywood. There are membranes and manufactured sheets that can let you get away with less, but for this project, ½-in. underlayment plywood was nailed to the ¾-in. subfloor. Use ring-shank nails every 6 in. in both directions throughout the floor to attach the underlayment.

SHOULD I TACKLE THIS MYSELF?

Pros

Once you understand the basics, tiling a floor is pretty straightforward. Just lay out, measure, cut, and install.

Cons

That said, if you plan on using a different pattern (such as diagonal), or if you want a border strip or inset tiles, I'd call in a pro. Also, I'd always count on using a tile saw, which may be more of an investment than you're willing to make for a tool you won't use that often. You can always rent a tile saw, but that can be a hassle in and of itself.

Easy, just count up the square feet you need to cover and divide by the size of the tile, right? Not so fast! If there is a lot of cutting to fit tile along walls, or to extend tile through a doorway into adjacent spaces, you can end up with a lot of waste. Look at your plan carefully, or better yet do a rough layout of the floor at the framing stage. If you need to do a lot of cutting, add 30 percent to 50 percent to your total. It's better to have a box of tile left over than to come up a few tiles short. In the latter case, you'll have to order additional tile and it can be next to impossible to blend the colors properly and seamlessly, and special ordering one or two boxes of tile can take weeks.

Measuring and layout

When working with tile in a basic square layout, the first thing to do is to establish a starting point, or more precisely, starting lines. Think of the tile in terms of blocks of about 2 ft. by 2 ft. For 12-in.-sq. tiles, that block would be 4 tiles; 8-in. tiles and the block would be 9 tiles; 6-in. tiles, 16 tiles; and so forth. When setting the tile, working in a 2-ft. square lets you work a little at a time so you don't get ahead of yourself.

Tile is made all over the globe, so tile measurements can vary significantly between manufacturers. Start by setting two tiles on the floor side by side with the space of the grout between them. On the floor shown here, the tiles with grout lines add up to $25\frac{7}{8}$ in. That measurement becomes the base for determining the layout. Next, measure the entire width you need to span and divide that length by your base length. Unless you're really lucky, you will end up with part of a tile left over. Determine where that piece should land to be the least noticeable. In this case, the tile was running under a vanity, so the most incon-

A tile saw is a must for doing tile installation quickly and efficiently. Most tile saws have a sliding table that you set the tile on securely and then push the tile into the blade. Tile saws use water to lubricate and cool the tile as it's being cut, and an abrasive blade with a diamond-encrusted edge. These tile-cutting blades won't rip you open like the toothed blades on most wood-cutting saws, but they should be treated with a lot of respect nonetheless. For cutting small areas or fine-tuning a cut, nippers are a must. Finally, you'll need a trowel with the appropriate-size teeth for the tile you're installing.

A tile saw is a huge help to make an installation go more quickly and efficiently. The saw uses a diamond-encrusted abrasive blade and sprays water on the cut to lubricate and cool the tile.

Place tiles together with the proper grout seam and measure the width. That figure becomes the base measurement for the layout.

spicuous place for a partial tile was along the vanity wall. With that in mind, we started our layout from the wall opposite the vanity wall. Using the same logic, we located a starting point in the perpendicular direction.

This project was complicated by the fact that the tile ran from the shower room into the vanity room. To snap the starting line, measurements had to be projected into the vanity room. So we measured and marked the starting point from the shower room wall. That point landed in the vanity room, so we marked the same measurements at both ends of the vanity room and snapped a chalkline through the marks. With the first line snapped, we then squared off the line in both directions and snapped a second line perpendicular to the first. A tile placed along the intersection of these two lines became the key tile and determined the placement of every tile in the space (see the top photo on p. 92). Without mortar, lay out tiles along the lines in both directions, spacing them with correct-size grout lines. Cut the partial tiles that you'll need along the wall and scribe the tiles to fit around the doorway as well (see the bottom photo on p. 92). When you've completed the dry fit to the wall and confirmed your layout, you're finally ready to set some tile.

Find the starting point along the snapped line and mark square lines from that point. Then snap a line through the square lines.

Using a multiple of the base measurement, mark the starting line for the tile. Make the measurement at both ends of the room and snap a chalkline perpendicular to the first line.

A tile placed at the intersection of the two snapped lines is the key tile and governs the placement of every tile on the floor (top). Without mortar, set tiles along the lines in both directions to confirm the layout (above).

Work a small area at a time

Before you start setting tile, you need to mix the thinset mortar. Be sure to ask your tile supplier which type of thinset to use with your particular tile. Certain types of tile have to be put down with a latex-modified thinset. The best way to mix the thinset is with a mixing paddle chucked into a heavy-duty drill. When the thinset is the proper consistency, let it slake or stand for 10 minutes or so, mix it again, and then start spreading it on the floor. Lift the tiles from your starting area, but leave the others for now, taking care not to disturb them.

For your first block of tiles, start at the snapped line and spread the thinset away from the line. Work the thinset both ways with the trowel until you have consistent full ridges left by the trowel teeth. The thinset should be an even depth in all areas. Now set the first tile. If the other dry-fit tiles are still in place, you should be able to position the first tile perfectly next to its neighbor. Press down on the tile firmly and wiggle it into position. This motion allows the tile to

Carefully lift the tile from a small area and spread thinset mortar evenly over the area, working away from the line. Note that the other dry-fit tiles are still in place.

Using the dry-fit tile as a guide, set the first tile into the mortar. Drop it into place, and then press down firmly on the tile and wiggle it slightly into position (far left).

Set the rest of the full tiles in that section and then fill in the cut tiles (left).

seat fully in the thinset. Follow with the next tile. Develop a setting pattern so that you place one edge of the tile close to the tile already set, align the tile, and then drop it into place. The "press and wiggle" motion then positions the tile exactly where it belongs.

When the block is complete, go back with a narrow putty knife and remove excess mortar from the gaps between the tiles. Give the tiles a quick wipe with a damp sponge to remove any excess mortar from the top surface. If there are any other tiles to complete the block, such as the cut tiles along the shower, put them in now. Place a framing square against the tiles you just installed and square a guide line down for your next block of four tiles. Spread thinset over that section, again working the thinset out from the line, and then set those four tiles. Continue this pattern until you've completed the space.

Square down from the installed tile to mark the placement for the next group of four tiles.

Working around obstacles

As you work across a bathroom floor, most of the cuts are straight and easy to make on the tile saw. Tiling around the toilet flange and supply line are more of a challenge. To scribe the cut, align the tile with the installed tiles and mark the boundaries of the flange. A triangle square can help with this step. Intersect the marks with a generous curve. A precise scribe is not necessary here, just a curve that roughly follows the curve of the flange. Now bring the tile out to your tile saw. Make a series of parallel cuts over to the curved line. If you hold the leading edge of the tile up slightly as you make your cuts, the saw blade cuts through the tile almost square, which eliminates fine tuning later on. The trick here is to hold the tile firmly against the fence on the table so that it doesn't move and bind the blade. If you're not comfortable with this maneuver, flip the tile over and finish the cuts from the back side.

To scribe the tile around the toilet flange, align the tile with already installed tiles and mark the perimeter of the flange using a triangle square. Connect the marks with a curve. Note that the scribe does not have to be perfect because it will be covered by the toilet.

To cut the curve, make a series of parallel cuts to the line. Holding the tile at an angle makes the saw cut through the tile more straight up and down.

When all the cuts are made, tap lightly on the "fingers" of material to break them off. Now use nibblers to cut the rest of the way to the line. Nibblers are like cutting pliers only with a blunt, hardened jaw made specifically to chomp through tile. The nibblers let you fine tune the scribe if necessary. Set the flange tile in place without mortar and scribe the fit for the supply pipe. Again work the tile in both directions to get the dimensions of the cut. This time the tile saw can be used to fine-tune the round cutout. Test the tile in place to make sure it fits, then spread the mortar and set the two scribed tiles along with the other two tiles in that block.

Grout time

The rest of the tile should go in fairly quickly and easily with all straight cuts on the saw. Continue the installation pattern you established earlier, working just a small area at a time (see the top photo on p. 96). If you get antsy and think you can set a bigger block at

Fine-tune the cut using nippers that nibble away at the edge of the cut a little at a time.

The cutout for the supply line can be done entirely on the tile saw, using the side of the blade to finish the curve.

The scribed pieces are then set into mortar.

From there the rest of the floor is easy, with all the cuts straight or square. Remember to continue working just a small area at a time to maintain control over the process.

Push the grout into the joints by keeping the float at an angle to the grout lines. Remove the excess grout with the float used as a scraper.

one time, avoid the temptation! Your anxiety will stay at a normal level and your floor will turn out better—guaranteed!

When all the tile is set, put tape across the doors to keep people from walking on the fresh tile. Let the tile sit at least overnight. Some professional tile setters allow the tile to sit for a couple of days.

Now comes the fun step of grouting or filling in the gaps between the tiles. Mix the grout according to the manufacturer's recommendation. A latex additive is often mixed in to give the grout more water resistance.

Apply the grout, working from the farthest corner toward the door. Set a small mound of grout on the tiles and with a rubber trowel (called a float), push the grout back and forth over the tiles. Keep the edge of the trowel at an angle to the grout lines to fill the gaps completely. Adjust the angle of the float as you grout as well. Start with an angle of about 45 degrees that pushes the grout into the gaps, and then finish with the trowel almost 90 degrees to the tile to scrape off the excess grout. Go over the tile with clean water and a sponge to continue removing the excess grout. Rinse the sponge often and change the water to keep it as clean as possible. Let the final milky haze dry on the tile. After the grout cures, remove the haze with a terrycloth rag. Finally, apply a coat of sealer if the tile you install requires it. Your tile supplier will let you know if sealer is necessary.

Float Angles for Grouting

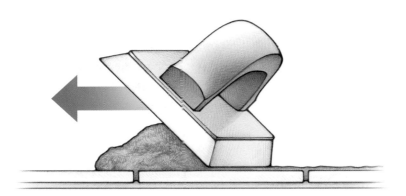

Keep the float at an angle To pack grout into joints, apply steady pressure with the float held at approximately 45° (above). A second pass with the float held closer to 90° will clean excess from the tile (below).

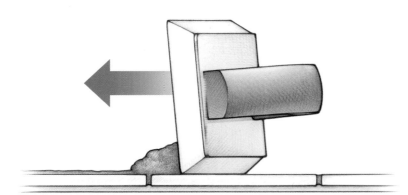

Let the grout dry and a white haze is left on the tile. Remove the haze with a terrycloth rag.

Wipe off the excess grout with a clean sponge and clear water. Keep rinsing the sponge and going over the tile until the grout has been removed.

Hanging Interior Doors

Once the flooring is in, the next step in the finishing process is hanging doors. This step should be done after the floors are installed (including tile floors), so that the jambs can be cut to length. And obviously the doors have to be in place before the door casing goes on. Because the baseboard butts into the casing, the doors have to be hung before the baseboard can be installed. So hanging doors is a critical link in the process of finishing the house.

This chapter deals with prehung doors, which have doors hinged to factory-made jambs. The two standard heights for doors are 6 ft. 8 in. (80 in.) and 6 ft. 6 in. (78 in.). In the trades these sizes are referred to as 6/8 ("six-eight") and 6/6 ("six-six"). These sizes are clearly spelled out on the plans so the framer can build the specified openings.

There are dozens of choices for prehung doors, such as solid slab, raised-panel, imitation raised panel, solid core, hollow core, and so on. The procedure for installing any of these choices is essentially the same.

Prepping for the Doors

Before the doors go in, it's probably a good idea to go around and check the jambs for level, both side-to-side in the rough opening and in the plane of the wall. Also check the floor. Quite often the floor on one side of the opening is slightly higher than the other. At this point there isn't much to be done if the wall is out of whack, but it's nice to know what you're up against before you begin. And if one side of the floor is higher, make your initial measurement from that side.

Put the right doors in the right rooms

When the truck arrives with your door order, you should have a good idea of exactly where each of the doors is going based on height, width, and whether it is a right-hand or a left-hand door. Depending on how you work, either label each door for where it's going or bring that door to its room. Some carpenters I know find it easier to number every door and its corresponding opening. That way there can be no location confusion if the door has been ordered properly.

Start with a level line

Begin by determining how high the door will sit in the opening. For a 6/8 door, the height measurement to the bottom edge of the head jamb is 80 in. plus ⁵⁄₈ in. or ¾ in. for clearance under the door. In this case, we measured up 80⅝ in. from the floor and marked that height on the wall (see the top left photo on p. 101). Level across the door opening at that height and mark the other side. That line is the bottom of the header jamb. Measure up from the floor and write down the height measurement for a reference. For those of you who think that writing down measurements is for rookies, remember the old adage: Measure twice, cut

SHOULD I TACKLE THIS MYSELF?

Pros

Hanging doors is one of the most basic steps in finish carpentry. If you follow the step-by-step procedure, it's really tough to mess up. If you've never hung a door, there is a steep learning curve to begin with. But once you've done a couple, it should be pretty smooth sailing. Plus, you use the same tools you'll need for a lot of the finish carpentry.

Cons

The person that might be discouraged from hanging doors is someone with no experience in finish carpentry or no desire to learn finish carpentry. The only other factor is time. An experienced carpenter who specializes in finish work can hang a door in 15 minutes. If you need to get this step done and out of the way quickly, you might want to call in a pro.

ESTIMATING MATERIALS

If you're at the stage for installing doors, the door "package" should have been ordered weeks ago. It normally takes that long for the lumber company to place the order with the manufacturer and to have the doors on hand ready to deliver. The door order is taken directly from the plans. The plans should spell out clearly the size of each door and the direction it swings. Doors cost more the wider and taller they are, but from there the costs are standard, unless you order a custom door. The width of a door is designated the same way as the height: a 2/8 door is 2 ft. 8 in. wide, or 32 in. wide. So, as an example, you'd order a door as six-eight by two-ten hinged left (see the sidebar on p. 100). Shorthand would be 6/8 by 2/10 L/H.

TOOLS NEEDED

- 2-ft. and 6-ft. levels
- Laser level (optional)
- Finish nailer
- Brad nailer
- Screw gun
- Compound miter saw

Right-Hand Versus Left-Hand Doors

Interior doors come in two basic configurations: Either the hinges are on the right or the hinges are on the left. But one of the mistakes often made is confusing right-hand doors and left-hand doors when ordering and when installing. It is something that has befuddled me since I began doing carpentry. I had to pound it into my head: With the door opening toward you, it's the side of the door with the knob. Another way to remember is to fold your arms, one on top of the other. Swing your forearm out in the direction that the door swings. Whichever arm you use determines right or left. Yet another method is called "butt-to-butt." Put your butt against the butt hinge side of the door, and whichever direction the door swings determines right or left. Still confused? You are in very good company, no doubt.

With the door opening toward you:

Knob on right = hinged right

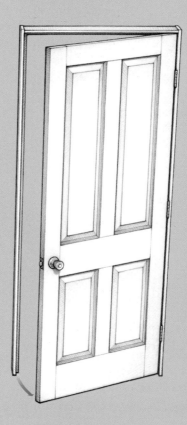

Knob on left = hinged left

Measure up to set the height of the door. The measurement is the height of the door plus clearance space. The line marks the bottom of the header jamb.

once. An adjunct to that notion is, measure once and write down the measurement so that you don't have to measure a second time!

Installing the Jambs

The first step is cutting the legs of the jambs to the right length. A word to the wise: Before you turn on the saw, review which way the door is to swing. It's one thing to order a door hinged on the wrong side, but it's another to mount the door so that it opens the wrong way, such as opening into the middle of the bedroom instead of opening against the wall of an adjoining

Level over and mark the other side of the rough opening (top). Write down the measurement as a reminder when you go to cut the jamb (above).

bathroom. If the side jambs are the same length, reversing a door after you cut it is no big deal. But if the lengths are different, you could end up with a door that doesn't have sufficient clearance and doesn't line up with the rest of the doors.

Cut the jamb assembly

Remove the door slab from the jamb assembly by pulling out the hinge pins. The assembly is very flimsy with the door taken out, so find a scrap of wood approximately the same length as the door is wide to act as a spreader. Put the spreader between the side jambs and grab the assembly on either side of the spreader, applying pressure to keep the spreader in place. Place the assembly on the miter-saw table sitting on one of the side jambs, and mark the length. Now make a square cut at the mark. Keeping the spreader in place, flip the door over and cut the other side jamb to length.

The jamb assembly is flimsy with the door removed, so a spreader bar keeps the side jambs properly spread for measuring (top) and for cutting (above).

Set the jamb assembly in the opening and check that the bottoms of the jambs are square to the floor.

Use a Laser Level to Set Door Heights

When I was making a living as a carpenter, lasers were something that scientists used in laboratories to make precision cuts through tough material such as stone and metal. Now lasers have become tools in the arsenals of most professional carpenters. Just a few years ago they were priced beyond the reach of most people in the trades, but as with many high-tech tools in this day and age, prices have dropped dramatically. At this point you can get a self-leveling laser for under $50. Using a laser sure would have saved me a ton of time and effort over the years.

The easiest way to mark heights using a laser level is with two crewmembers. Choose a door opening and measure up from the floor on one side of the opening. Have the first crewmember hold the laser at that height. The laser automatically emits a perfectly level line around the rest of the room. While the laser is held at the proper height, the other crewmember can go to each door opening and mark the height on both sides.

Before installing the jamb assembly, check the header to make sure it's level (top). Set the hinge side of the assembly against the rough opening and use a 6-ft. level to check for plumb (right).

When both side jambs are cut, carefully bring the jamb assembly to the opening. First check to make sure the jamb is square to the floor in the opening on both sides (see the right photo on p. 102). Next, check the header to make sure it is sitting perfectly level. Put the hinge side against the side of the rough opening to make sure it's plumb (see the photos on p. 103). Typically you try to install the door roughly centered in the opening, but if you find that the opening is out of plumb you may have to compensate in order to be able to plumb the opposite side jamb.

Shim and nail the hinge jamb

Although some production door hangers on the West Coast pooh-pooh the idea of using shims for installing doors, I've never successfully hung a door without shims. The most common shim material in this area is white cedar shingles. White cedar shims come in handy for a variety of uses, and most carpenters I know keep a bundle on hand at all times. Grab a handful of shingles and cut them down to $1\frac{1}{2}$-in. to 2-in. widths. To cut them, just score one side with a utility knife and then snap them at the score line. The gradually tapered profile of the shingles makes them perfect for micro-adjustment of the jambs. Shims are used in pairs so the taper cancels itself out, which brings the jamb out evenly from the rough opening and gives it uniform backing for the nails. For wider gaps, you may need to use an additional pair of shims. If the side of the rough opening is twisted at all, using

White cedar shingles make the best shims. To make the shims, first score the shingle with a utility knife every $1\frac{1}{2}$ in. to 2 in. (top). The scored shingle can then be broken into individual shims by hand (right).

two shims on one side and one on the other can compensate for the discrepancy.

To start, slip shims in from both sides of the jamb just below the top hinge position. Slice them together evenly (the same amount from each side) until the gap between the jamb and the rough opening is where you'd like it. (Again, I always try to center the assembly in the rough opening, but if the sides of the opening aren't plumb, you need to adjust the gap accordingly.) Make sure that the jamb is even with the plane of the wallboard on both sides of the wall, and maintain pressure on the jamb to keep the shims in place. Drive or shoot a 2½-in. finish nail through the center of the jamb, through the shims, and into the side of the rough opening. Drive finish nails on either side of center as well.

With the top secure, insert shims just below the level of the bottom hinge. Adjust the shims in or out until the jamb is perfectly plumb. A 6-ft. level is a must for this procedure. A shorter level is apt to record small variations in the actual jamb rather than give you an overall reading of plumb (see the drawing on p. 106). When you've got the jamb perfectly plumb top

Insert a pair of opposing shims just below the top hinge location and then drive a nail to hold the jamb and the shims in position.

Shimming the jamb

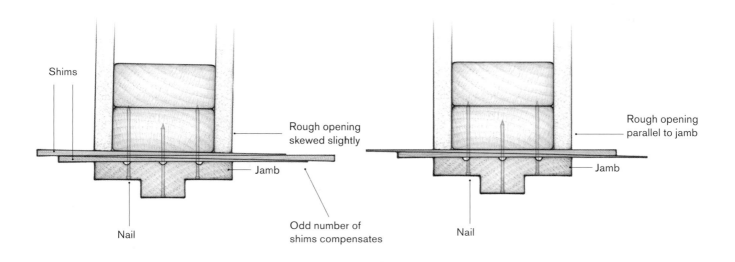

Shims

Rough opening skewed slightly

Jamb

Nail

Odd number of shims compensates

Rough opening parallel to jamb

Jamb

Nail

Using a 6-ft. Level

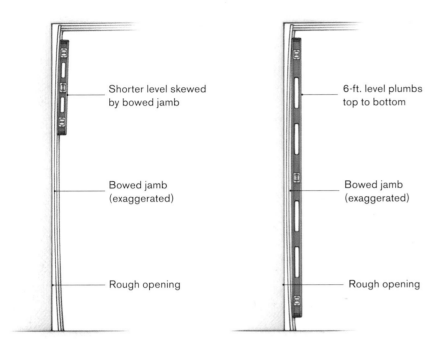

Shorter level skewed by bowed jamb

Bowed jamb (exaggerated)

Rough opening

6-ft. level plumbs top to bottom

Bowed jamb (exaggerated)

Rough opening

TIP

Magnetic Levels

If you need to purchase a 6-ft. level, get one that has a magnetic edge. The level sticks to the hinges, leaving your hands free to adjust the shims and drive the nails. The magnetic levels are a little more expensive, but the time and effort you save on hanging a couple of doors will more than make up the difference.

Plumb down with a 6-ft. level and adjust the shims to hold the jamb in place (left). Nail through the jamb and the shingles to hold the bottom in place (above).

to bottom, drive finish nails to secure the bottom of the jamb through the shims.

Now insert shims just below the middle hinge. Keep the 6-ft. level in place and adjust the shims until the middle of the jamb is perfectly in line with the top and bottom. When it's right, nail the jamb at that point as well. Beware of warped or twisted jambs. A couple of years back I bought a door from a local building supplier's bargain counter. I should have known when I saw a 12d common nail driven through the jamb to hold the door in place. But the door was inexpensive and I figured I could handle any differences. When I popped the 12d nail out, both jambs were warped and twisted—a bargain indeed! In that case I ended up shimming the door every 8 in. to make the jamb perfectly straight and plumb—maybe more work than it was worth.

Now plumb the latch jamb

With the hinge jamb set, insert shims on the opposite side just below the header jamb and push the shims together until they make a snug fit. Drive one finish nail to keep the jamb aligned with the plane of the wall and to keep the shims from falling while you secure the rest of the jamb. The latch jamb (or strike jamb) is adjusted according to the gap between the door and the jamb, so you now need to put the door back on its hinges.

There's a bit of an art to getting a door back on its hinges. It's rare that all three hinges slide into place all at once. In a more typical scenario, you slide the top hinge into place first, and then slip in the hinge pin to keep it aligned. Now go to the middle hinge and do the same. If one of the hinges is reluctant to slide into place, give it a light hammer tap as persuasion.

Close the door and you're ready to shim and nail the opposite jamb. A helper makes this stage of the

Beware of Loose Hinges

With today's paint-grade doors made from composite materials, screws are notorious for stripping out their holes. The hinge leaf is then loose, and a screw head sticking out slightly can change the way the door sits in the jamb. Inspect every hinge for loose or stripped screws. Hinge screws are usually just 1 in. long. Drive a 2-in. or 2½-in. screw to replace the stripped screw, but make sure it's the same gauge screw with the same diameter head. Larger-gauge screws with bigger heads won't tighten flush with the hinge surface and can affect the way the door closes as much as the bad screw.

Inspect the door for stripped screws that can keep the door from closing properly. Replace any stripped screw with a longer screw that is the same gauge.

process go much more quickly. Have that person insert a shim 6 in. to 8 in. from the bottom of the door while you do the same from your side. This time, adjust the shims in or out until the gap between the door and the jamb is exactly the same at the bottom as it is at the top. Use your steel rule to make sure the door is flush with the plane of the wall. While keeping pressure on the jamb to hold the shims in place, open the door and nail through the shims in the middle as well as on both sides of the jamb.

Close the door again and insert a third pair of shims just below the striker plate location. Once again adjust the shims according to the gap between the door and the jamb. When that location is set, nail through the shims there as well as at the top where you began. Because the first set of shims on the latch side was very close to the top of the jamb, add a fourth pair of shims midway between the top two sets of shims. Go back and make sure the jambs have received three nails at every shim location.

Give the door a final check for plumb. The final step is cutting the shims back. Be sure to angle your utility knife so that you cut the shim behind the plane of the wall and the door jamb.

Use a metal rule to make sure the jamb is in the plane of the adjacent wall (above).

Open the door and drive three nails through the jamb and shims and into the rough-opening framing (left).

Trim the shims with a utility knife, making sure they break off below the surface of the wall (above).

Shim and nail the jamb just below the strike location (top left), and then insert and nail a final pair of shims about two-thirds of the way up the door (left).

Adjusting a Door after Hanging and Trimming

No matter how careful you are, a door can go out of adjustment during the process of trimming and finishing. This was especially true before pneumatics became commonplace. Driving nails into the casing with a hammer made the door assembly go through the stress of a lot of pounding. The most common problem is the latch side of the door dropping down in the opening. And the easiest fix is driving a long screw at the top hinge location. The screw goes through to the framing and pulls the door back where it needs to be.

My solution was always to take out a hinge screw and drive the long screw in its place. But this solution has a couple of drawbacks. First, it's difficult to find long screws in the same finish as the hinges and hinge screws, so the replacement screw always sticks out like a sore thumb. The second problem is with our friends, the painters. It's always best to remove the doors along with the hinges when it comes time to paint. If the painter removes the hinge and one of the screws is long, chances are that person will lose track of where the long screw belongs. A better solution is to unscrew the hinge from the jamb and to drive the long adjustment screw behind the hinge location. That way the screw can stay put during the rest of the finishing process, and it's invisible when the hinge is put back on.

While on the *Fine Homebuilding* staff I was lucky enough to work with Gary Katz. In addition to his amazing skills as a finish carpenter, Gary spent a good deal of time as a door hanger. In an article he did on retrofitting exterior doors, Gary offered a couple of

If adjustment is needed after the door is cased, drive a long screw behind the hinge where it will be concealed.

To move the door away from the opposite jamb, bend the hinge barrels with a crescent wrench.

tips on tweaking a door in its opening. These tips can be used to adjust any hinged door.

Often it is necessary to move the top of the door one way or the other to create a perfectly even gap between the edge of the door and the latch jamb. If you need to close the gap on the latch side, place the square end of a nailset between the leaves of the hinge and close the door gently. The nailset spreads the hinge, which then moves the door over and reduces the gap.

If you need to widen the gap by moving the door toward the hinge side, pull the top hinge pin until it barely engages the top barrel. Tighten a small crescent wrench around each of the barrels and bend the hinge slightly toward the latch side, which widens the gap on the latch side.

A Few Notes about Other Types of Doors

The process for installing doors in rough openings is pretty much the same regardless of the type of door. For doors without hinges, such as bifold doors or sliding doors for a closet, install the preassembled jamb one side at a time. You can choose which side goes in first. If the opening is more than 3 ft. wide, I'd recommend shimming or blocking between the header jamb and the top of the rough opening to keep the jamb level and to prevent it from sagging. I've heard of carpenters who just depend on the casing to hold the header straight, but blocking is good insurance, especially if the header jamb is to carry the door's weight, as with sliding doors.

With the doors hung, we can now proceed to the door casing, which I cover in the next chapter.

The door can be easily adjusted to sit properly in the opening. To move the door toward the opposite jamb, place a nailset between the hinge leaves and close the door gently. The hinge will bend slightly and move the door toward the strike jamb.

Window and Door Trim

If you've been building your own home, you've watched the inside of the house progress in levels of finish. First the openings for windows and doors are framed, then surrounded by drywall. At that point you still had the ragged edges of the drywall and 2×s defining the openings. Next you hung doors in their openings, while the windows still awaited their finish. The next stage is window and door trim to cover and finish the spaces between the jambs and the drywall.

The window and door trim is significant because of the level of finish it represents. But also the choice of trim and trim style dictates the feeling and "flavor" of the home. When I built my little raised ranch, I'd seen only ranch- and colonial-style casing, and thought that anything else had to be custom ordered. I was amazed that there were many other stock choices out there for trim. I actually opted for a flat, square-edged casing with slightly eased edges to give the house a more contemporary look. When I re-cased the windows in my Connecticut home, I "built" my own molding profile. I started by cutting a bead in the edge of flat square stock. Then I added a bullnose frame around that and base cap molding between the two. The bottom line is that I ended up with an attractive molding that I thought fit both the age and the style of the home.

At the project I photographed for this chapter, the doors and windows were trimmed using a stock molding called "Marblehead." The molding was milled from paint-grade poplar, a common and fairly inexpensive choice around these parts. If you haven't decided on a choice for casing, visit your local lumber company. You may be surprised at the stock offerings to choose from.

Trimming Windows

There are two basic methods for trimming windows: either with a window sill or without. The latter is also known as a "picture frame" method because the trim is a square or rectangle, just like a picture frame. When a window sill is used, the trim lands on a horizontal sill in the shape of an upside-down "U." An apron finishes off the trim below the sill. The latter method is usually specified here in New England because the sill gives you a surface to set things on, such as small plants, or a place for the cat to sit and watch birds. The sill method is a bit more time-consuming because of

TOOLS NEEDED
- Sliding compound miter saw
- Jigsaw
- Router or router table
- Finish nailer, brad nailer, and pinner
- Levels

SHOULD I TACKLE THIS MYSELF?

Pros

If you enjoy carpentry—especially finish carpentry—I'd say, absolutely. This step is challenging and fun, and you get to use a variety of tools and carpentry techniques.

Cons

The only reasons I can see not to do this step are time and lack of experience. If you are in a rush to get the house finished, or if you're on a strict deadline to finish, a professional finish carpenter is probably going to get the job done much more quickly and efficiently.

ESTIMATING MATERIALS

Usually the company you use to provide the doors is the same company that provides the trim, so estimating is not a factor. Molding is usually sold by the foot, and most lumber companies will prepare molding "packages" for each window, with lengths rounded up to the nearest 6 in. for the jambs, header, and apron. The packages come neatly bundled together. Note any finished openings without doors that need to be trimmed. Order 7-footers for the jambs and whatever length you need for the headers—and don't forget that there are two sides to every door so make sure you order double. It's a good idea to get a few extra lengths for goof fixes and unanticipated uses.

Window trim without a sill is usually called picture frame because the casing surrounds the window in a rectangular shape.

The reveal is the amount of material left exposed before the next layer of material goes on. Here a ¼-in. reveal is marked to the edge of the extension jambs.

To mark the length of the sill, add the reveals, the width of the casing, plus the amount that you want the sill to extend past the casing, and measure that distance from the inside edge of the jamb.

the extra trim piece involved, and it's the trim method that is detailed in this chapter.

Start with the sills

Because all of the flat trim lands on or springs from the sills either above or below, the sills are the first pieces of window trim to go in. But before they do, mark the reveal at the top corners as well as the middle and the bottom of the side jambs. The reveal is the amount of wood that is left exposed when the next layer of trim is installed. In this case, a ¼-in. reveal was left on the edge of the actual window jamb for placement of the extension jambs, and an additional ¼-in. reveal on the extension jambs was left for the window casing. In the interest of time, it makes sense to go around and mark the reveal on all the windows before proceeding to the sills.

The next step is to mark the width of the sills on the drywall on either side of the window. For this project there were two ¼-in. reveals, a 3½-in.-wide trim, and an overhang of 1 in., for a total of 5 in. So at the bottom edge of the window, we measured out and marked 5 in. from the inside edge of the jambs on both sides. The distance between the two marks is the length of the sill. Cut a piece of sill stock to that length plus a couple of inches and bring it to the window. Sill stock is typically thicker than standard trim, in this case 5/4 or a full 1 in. thick. A dado on the inside half of the stock allows it to sit on the sill portion of the factory jamb.

Hold the sill against the drywall close to position with one leg. First mark the overall length of the sill. Now measure the distance that the sill has to move in to hit the sash or the trim stop in front of the sash. Holding your rule against the factory side jamb, mark that distance from the back of the sill stock. The sill has to step around the side jamb, so mark the depth of the jamb on the sill next. Mark the same distance near the overall length mark as well. Connect the marks, square down from the overall length marks, and you're ready to cut.

Six-Inch Metal Ruler

ESSENTIAL TOOLS

I was a little surprised that none of the finish carpenters on this job wore tool belts. When I asked about it, they said that it was too easy to swing around and have a hammer head or different tool mar a finished surface. So they just brought a few tools to each area they worked in. One tool that each one of them used more often than any other was a 6-in. stainless-steel ruler. One side has eighths and sixteenths etched on it whereas the other side has thirty-seconds and sixty-fourths. When you get down to tolerances this small, a measuring tape is not dependable. A cool feature is having measurements marked on the ends of the ruler as well. These guys didn't just use these handy tools for measuring, they also made great tools for scraping off excess glue or adhesive. And the thin blade meant that they could clean out even the narrowest profile. At around $5 each, these tools earn their keep pretty quickly.

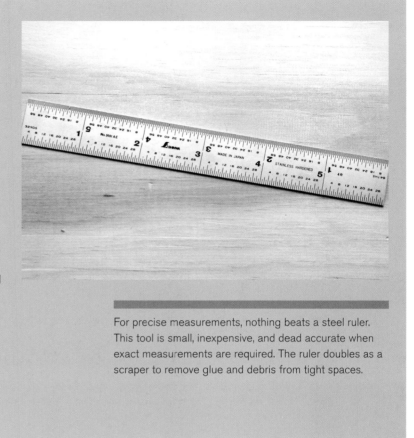

For precise measurements, nothing beats a steel ruler. This tool is small, inexpensive, and dead accurate when exact measurements are required. The ruler doubles as a scraper to remove glue and debris from tight spaces.

The best and safest way to make the cuts is to make the ripcuts first with a tablesaw or jigsaw. Then make the crosscuts with a compound miter saw. Tilt the sill stock toward you slightly and the sawblade can cut all the way through your ripcuts. Next, round over the ends of the sill with a router, and sand the ends smooth. Test fit the sill in the window. Pay special attention to the last couple of inches on either end of the sill to make sure it fits tightly against the drywall—those joints will be visible. Then take the sill out and apply construction adhesive to both the factory sill of the window and the back of the sill. When it cures, the adhesive will be stronger than the nails you use to attach the sill. Set the sill in place carefully without smearing the adhesive. Then nail the sill into place with a finish nailer (see the photos on pp. 116–117). Nail through the sill into the factory sill, then use long finish nails to attach the ends of the sills through the drywall and into the studs.

Holding the sill stock against the window opening, first mark the length of the sill. From the back edge of the stock, measure the distance to the window stop. Now draw a line for the inside of the jamb and mark the distance you measured on that line. Mark the same distance out from the end measurement point, and connect the two marks.

After ripping the cutout portion with a jigsaw, use a miter saw to make the crosscuts. While maintaining constant firm pressure on the workpiece against the saw fence, tip the work forward slightly to complete the cut.

With a roundover bit mounted in a router, round the ends of the sill (left), and then sand the ends smooth with a vibrating sander (below left).

Apply construction adhesive to the sill jamb as well as to the sill itself. Then slide the sill into position carefully so you don't smear the adhesive (below).

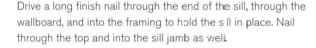

Drive a long finish nail through the end of the sill, through the wallboard, and into the framing to hold the sill in place. Nail through the top and into the sill jamb as well.

Extension jambs build the factory jambs out to the same plane as the surrounding wallboard. The extension jambs align with the reveal marks you made before, and are then nailed. Make another set of reveal marks on the extension jambs for the casing.

Extension jambs

In all my years as a carpenter, I've never seen a house where the factory jambs on the windows are perfectly flush with the face of the drywall without some sort of modification. That modification usually comes in the form of extension jambs, or strips of wood that nail onto the factory jambs to build them out or extend them out to the plane of the drywall. Some window manufacturers make their own extension jambs that are rabbeted into the factory jamb, but even those need to be ripped to fit. Most often, extension jambs are the strips of wood ripped out of 1-in. stock to whatever thickness is needed.

The thickness of the extension jambs is a factor of the framing thickness plus the thickness of the drywall. In many parts of the country, including southeastern New England where I live, shear panels are specified for certain walls. The panels are created in part by adding a layer of plywood to the inside of the framing. The drywall then goes on top of the plywood. Extension jambs in these walls have to be thicker to make up for the plywood. Place a scrap of wood flat against the drywall and measure to the factory jamb for the thickness. Measure at a number of places around the window, especially at the corners, where compound may have built up. Measurements should be within $1/16$ in. or so. High spots can be "flattened" with a hammer if necessary. When you've ripped the extension jambs, cut the sides to length and nail them in. They can extend past the top of the window slightly if need be. Nail them to the reveal marks you made earlier. Cut the extension jamb for the top of the window and nail it in place. As a final step, mark the reveal for the window casing on the extension jambs.

Make a 45-degree angle cut exactly at the measurement mark.

With a slot-cutting router bit and a router table, cut the slot for the corner biscuit.

Window casing

The next step is building the window casing. There are three pieces: the two side casings and the header casing. Some carpenters like to make the sides first and then the header, but the crew on this job did one side, then the header, then the second side, sort of working their way around the window. The first step in either case is cutting one of the sides.

Make a square cut on the end that sits on the sill and then set the casing in place, aligning it with the reveal marks. Mark the top reveal on the edge of the casing. This mark is the inside corner of the casing. On the sliding compound miter saw, set the bevel angle at 0 degrees and the miter angle at 45 degrees. Don't go for the line right off, even if you have a laser guide on your miter saw. Instead, start the cut about $\frac{1}{16}$ in. long and move the board over a hair at a time until the blade lands perfectly on the mark. (By the way, be sure to make all of your marks with a sharp pencil. If the mark is $\frac{1}{16}$ in. wide, it defeats the purpose of cutting to the line.)

Test fit the piece to make sure the length is right and then make a biscuit slot in the end. Recall that the flooring installers used a freehand router with a slotting cutter to cut new butt end grooves. The finish carpenters use the same type of cutter, only in a router mounted in a router table. They also use a smaller bearing to allow the cutter to plunge in deeper to make room for the biscuit. I've always preferred a router table because it lets you use two hands to control the piece of wood that you're routing. The finished side casing can then be nailed into place. Along the inside edge, use brad nails, which are less likely to split the wood. Nail through the bead every 8 in. or so. Use a finish nailer to attach the outside edge. On this side, drive the nails through a flat part of the profile so that the holes can be filled easily.

Cut a 45-degree angle on one end of the header casing and test-fit it against the installed side casing. Be sure to align the piece on the reveal marks before checking the angle. At this point it's easy to make a slight adjustment to the angle of the cut. Go for a perfectly tight fit. On this particular window, the drywall stuck out slightly, causing the header casing to rock back and forth instead of lying flat against the drywall and the extension jamb. Time for my favorite trick: drywall excavation! With the header casing in place, draw a light line along the top. Use the claw end of the hammer to take out the offending drywall, staying at least 1 in. or so away from the line. The header casing should now lay completely flat and you can mark the length at the side reveal mark. If you're like me, it's not hard to get confused as you walk

Nail the side jamb into place using a brad nailer along the thinner inner edge (left) and a finish nailer along the outside edge (above). Drive the finish nails into a flat part of the casing profile to make filling the holes easier.

Make a 45-degree angle cut on the header casing and test-fit the miter joint with the side casing by holding the header casing on the reveal marks.

Sometimes the drywall interferes with the casing lying flat. Draw a line on the drywall for the top of the casing and remove or pulverize the drywall so it is no longer in the way.

between the window and the saw, so get in the habit of making a slash mark beyond the mark to indicate the direction of the cut. When you've cut the other side of the header, make the biscuit slots and set the piece aside.

The opposite side casing is next, and you follow the same process of squaring the end, marking the length, and cutting the 45-degree angle. Test-fit the side casing and header casing together, again adjusting the angle slightly if necessary. Don't forget to cut the slot for the biscuit and then nail in the opposite side as you did with the first side. Now spread yellow carpenter's glue

on the ends of the header casing, making sure to get plenty of glue in the biscuit slots. Insert the biscuits and distribute the glue evenly on the cut end of the board and also on the biscuit itself. Most carpenters I know just use their fingers to spread the glue, but at the boatyard I got used to using small disposable brushes called "acid brushes." They saved me from making a mess, and I didn't wipe my gluey fingers on my pants nearly as much.

Install the header casing by sliding one end in at a time. Pull down tightly on the corners and nail the casing the same way you did the sides. Wipe the excess

Mark the length of the header casing, cut it to length, and set aside (above left).

Cut and install the opposite side jamb the same as the first side (above).

Tolerances

Most good finish carpenters work to tolerances of 1/64 in. even with paint-grade material. If you're working on your own house, you can decide what is "good enough." Sometimes, the extra time to achieve those tolerances is out of the question. Also decide where to put your effort to achieve the highest tolerances. A 1/64-in. gap may be much more apparent in a corner miter than where the casing meets the sill or the floor.

glue with a finger or scrape it off with the 6-in. ruler. Wipe the joint with a damp cloth and give the joint a light sanding with 220-grit sandpaper.

The apron comes last

The most efficient, if boring, way to trim windows is to do a room at a time or an entire floor at a time. With the finish crew I worked with on this project, one crewmember went through an entire floor installing window sills. Then a second crewmember followed installing the extension jambs and casing. Finally, all the aprons were installed at once. This strategy keeps one person working the same job throughout a floor before switching to the next job. The result is a more efficient use of time and effort.

The final piece of window trim is the apron, which fits below the window sill. For appearance' sake, the ends of the apron should line up with the outside edges of the side casing, so just measure from one side to the other for the length of the apron. The ends of the apron are finished with "returns." Instead of an

Slip the header casing into position one end at a time. Pull down firmly to close the corner joints completely and then nail it in place with the same nails as the side casing.

Spread wood glue evenly on the mating surface of the joint. Be sure to get glue in the biscuit slot and to spread glue on both sides of the biscuit.

Wipe the excess glue off the joint with a damp cloth and sand the joint lightly with 220-grit paper.

unattractive square cut, the ends are mitered and tiny wedges of the material are glued on that "return" the apron back to the wall. The most difficult and nerve-racking part of this process is cutting the tiny wedges. Remember that it's much easier to cut slivers off of a bigger piece of wood, so to cut the returns start with a length of casing stock a few inches longer than you need for the apron.

Set the bevel angle on the saw to 45 degrees this time and keep the miter angle at 0 degrees. With the casing stock lying flat on the saw table, make a 45-degree cut in each end of the casing. Now reset the

bevel angle to 0 degrees and flip the stock upside down. Hold the top of the apron tight against the fence, which means keeping the bottom or bead edge of the apron elevated slightly off the saw table. Bring the sawblade down right along the inside line of the bevel cut. The little wedge should fall away safely without flying away.

Having cut the returns safely, now you can cut the actual aprons. Make a 45-degree bevel cut on one end and then hook your tape to the longest part of the profile (usually the top). Mark the length you need, tip the head of the saw to a 45-degree bevel in the

Measure from one side casing to the other for the overall length of the apron.

To cut the return pieces for the apron, first make a bevel cut in the ends of the apron stock.

With the stock face held parallel to the saw table, the small wedge should fall safely away from the blade. The return piece has a 45-degree bevel that mates to the end of the apron.

Flip the stock over and, holding the back of the stock parallel to the plane of the saw table, make a square cut along the inside line of the bevel cut.

opposite direction, and cut the other end. Now it's just a matter of gluing on the returns. Slather yellow carpenter's glue on the angled side of the little wedge and slide it into position on the end of the apron. (By the way, if you slide the wedge into position with the apron on a flat surface, the surface helps to align the piece.) Holding the wedge carefully in position, drive a couple of pins into the wedge to hold it in place while the glue dries (see the top photo on p. 124). Go over the joint lightly with sandpaper and the apron is ready for installation.

Adding the back bevel with a tablesaw is the final step in preparing the aprons. To install an apron, first put a bead of construction adhesive along the top of the apron as well as on the back (see the top photo on p. 125). To keep the surrounding drywall clean, get the

Now cut the apron to length with a 45-degree bevel on each end.

Glue the return in place and secure it with light-gauge pin nails.

apron as close to position as possible before pressing it against the wall and up against the sill.

With the apron properly aligned and held in position, nail it off completely with a finish nailer. Along the top edge of the apron, angle the nails upward slightly to draw the apron up to the sill. Use nails long enough to go through the trim, through the drywall, and into the framing. Look for any gaps that might still be there between the sill and the apron. Some carpenters just nail through the sill into the apron, but every time I tried that, I'd end up with a nail poking out in some inappropriate and hard-to-hide place. As seen in the top photo on p. 126, this crew used sliding bar clamps to draw the two surfaces together until the glue had a chance to cure (a couple of hours). Top-of-the-line construction adhesive is quite tenacious and is sufficient for holding the joint together.

The Back Bevel: A Finish Carpenter's Best Friend

I was always frustrated trying to get the edge of one trim element to fit tight against another. I'd use clamps, screws, and other medieval methods and still end up with gaps. Then I was looking at some finish work by a friend, Rob Turnquist, who is an amazing carpenter. He told me his secret: the back bevel. For these window aprons, the crew cut a 5-degree bevel angled back from the top front edge on a tablesaw. (Rob used to make his back bevel with a razor-sharp low-angle block plane.) This slight angle creates room for glue as well as for any minor flaws that might cause a gap, and instead of trying to mate a 3/4-in.-wide flat surface, just a thin knife edge actually makes contact with the underside of the sill. The result is a tight, professional-looking joint.

A back bevel on the top of the apron allows for a tight fit under the sill. Set the tablesaw blade at 5 degrees and carefully shave off the angle.

Apply construction adhesive along the top and back of the apron for the strongest joint.

Site-Built Alignment Tool

An easily made tool helps to align the apron perfectly with the edge of the casing above the sill. Take a scrap of 1× (in this case a piece of baseboard stock) about 10 in. long. With a jigsaw, cut a "U" shape out of the middle of one edge. To align the apron, press the tool against the jamb casing with the U going around the overhang of the sill. Slide the apron over until it meets the bottom of the tool. Drive a quick nail to hold it in position.

A shop-made tool aligns the end of the apron perfectly with the edge of casing above.

Nail the apron with finish nails into the framing. Angle nails along the top slightly to draw the apron up to the sill.

If more persuasion is needed to close the gap between the sill and the apron, draw the two together with a clamp. Keep the clamp on for a few hours until the adhesive cures.

Where two windows are joined together, a mullion strip finishes the joint between them. The stock for this strip is milled thinner so it fits in behind the plane of the casing.

Mullions

The first time I heard the word "mullions" on a jobsite, a wiseguy crewmember said, "No thanks, I'll have the green beans." As much as the word sounds like a vegetable, it actually describes the joint between two windows that are joined edge to edge. The doubled up or "mulled" windows in this project were actually separated by doubled 2×s, which required a finished mullion over 5 in. wide. The extension jambs were left off on either side of the mullion to allow the mullion trim to sit back behind the plane of the casing. The mullion trim still had to be thinner than standard stock; in this case, about $\frac{1}{2}$ in. thick. The safest way to make thinner stock is with a portable thickness planer.

When you've made your stock at the proper thickness, sit a squared end on the sill and line up the mullion with the reveal marks. Now mark the length to the bottom edge of the header casing. Cut the mullion and test-fit it in place. With this particular project there was a void between the framing and the backside of the mullion. Because the mullion stock is so thin, blocking was needed to provide (nailing) support behind it. To determine the thickness of the blocking, use a straight piece of wood as a bridge between the jambs and measure to the framing. When you determine the block thickness you need, rip stock to that thickness and cut the blocks to length. Nail blocks in every foot or so onto the framing between the windows. Then spread construction adhesive on the blocks as well as along the top and bottom of the opening. The trim is then installed and nailed into place with a brad nailer.

To support the mullion strip from behind, add blocks between the factory jambs. To measure the thickness needed, bridge the jambs with a straight piece of wood and measure to the framing.

Door Casing

Installing door casing is very similar to window casing, only without the sill and apron. Even so, it's a good idea to go over the process step by step. Just as with the window casing, the first step is to mark the reveal. A small adjustable square works well for this step. Just slide the adjustable shoulder section to the size of the reveal and secure it there. Then butt the shoulder to the jamb surface and mark the reveal (see the top photo on p. 128). Also check for places where the surrounding drywall sticks out beyond the jamb. In carpentry terms we would say that the drywall is "proud of the jamb." These areas can keep the casing from lying flat against the jamb and the drywall. With a hammer, gently tap the drywall to pulverize the gypsum and make room for the casing.

Nail the blocks in and then apply construction adhesive to them.

Nail the mullion strip into place with brads.

Mark the reveal for the door casing as you did for the window casing. An adjustable square set at the space of the reveal is a good tool for this task.

Square the side casing to the floor

Start by making a square cut on the end of one of the side casings. Set the casing in place, align the edge with the reveal marks, and check to make sure the bottom edge of the casing meets the flooring precisely. If the angle is off, you can scribe the bottom of the casing with a pencil lying flat on the floor, and then adjust the cut.

When you're satisfied with the bottom joint, hold the casing in place and mark the length. Cut the 45-degree miter at the mark and rout a slot for the corner biscuit, just as you did for the window casing. Then nail the casing into place. Use a brad nailer for the thinner inside edge of the casing and a finish nailer for the thicker outside edge. Cut a 45-degree miter on the end of the header casing and test-fit it against the first side casing. Again, adjust the angle of the cut if the casings don't meet perfectly, and realize that these angle adjustments are usually half of a degree or less.

Next, mark the length of the header casing, but cut it 1/8 in. long. The extra length gives you some wiggle room to adjust the angle if necessary. As with the first side casing, square the bottom and make sure the joint is satisfactory before marking and cutting it to length.

In places where the drywall sticks out too far, tap it gently with a hammer to pulverize the gypsum so the casing will lay flat.

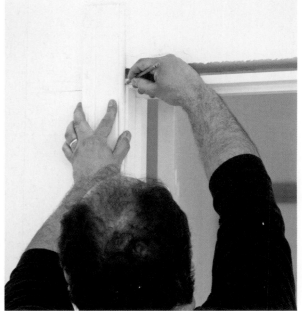

Cut one end of the casing so it sits flat against the floor and then mark the length at the reveal line. Cut the casing to length and rout a slot in the end for a biscuit.

Nail it in place, keeping it precisely on the reveal marks. Now set the header in place to check the angle of the other corner. Remember that you cut the piece slightly long, so line up the bottom parallel with the reveal, and make sure that both miters are perfect. Then cut the header to the mark you made earlier.

Slather glue on the mating surface as well as in the groove for the biscuit. Insert the biscuit and smear glue on both sides of it. Gluing every joint is a critical step in the finishing process. The glue keeps the joint together over the long run throughout the life of the house. Slip the header into place, letting the biscuits slide into their slots on the side jambs. Close the joint completely by squeezing down on the casing. When the joint is closed completely, there should be glue oozing out of it. Nail the header casing the same as the side casing, with brads in the thin edge and finish nails in the outer edge. When you're done, drive a brad at each corner to help hold it together while the glue sets up. Wipe up excess glue with a damp rag and give the joint a light sanding with 220-grit sandpaper (see the left photos on p. 130).

Occasionally, nails just aren't enough to draw the casing tight against the jamb. In these cases, use a

As with the window casing, cut, fit, and prepare the header casing, and then cut and install the opposite side casing.

Nail in the casing with brads on the inside edge and finish nails along the outside edge.

Glue the ends of the header casing and the biscuits and squeeze the header casing into place.

Nail off the face of the header casing and then secure the corners with brads to hold them together while the glue dries.

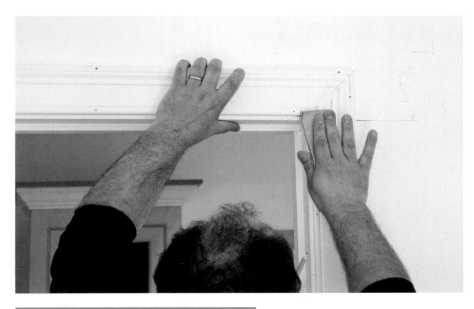

Wipe off the excess glue with a damp rag and sand the joint smooth with 220-grit paper.

If there are still gaps between the jamb and the casing, draw the casing in with a clamp and drive additional nails at an angle. Use a scrap of wood to protect the casing from getting marred by the clamp.

clamp (with a wood block to protect the casing) to close any gap. Then drive additional brads at a slight angle to keep the gap from opening back up.

Too many doorways, not enough room

Among the hardest areas to design, frame, and then trim are hallways. Architects love to minimize the size of hallways to maximize the size of the adjoining rooms. The problem is that the more you shrink a hallway, the closer the doors get to each other. It's not uncommon to have multiple bedrooms, bathrooms, and closets all opening into the same limited hallway space. The result is that the doorways and casings get jammed together, often without enough space for full-width casing between them. Or there is just a fraction of an inch left between adjacent casings. Corners are also notorious tight spots. Done wrong and they are nearly impossible to paint. Done right and the trim is seamless and looks like you'd planned that configuration all along.

If you have a tight corner where two door casings intersect, the best option is to glue and nail a strip of wood onto the edge of one of the casings after you've cut it to length. Let the strip extend past the top and bottom of the casing and trim the strip to length after the glue has dried. The strip allows the casing to extend all the way into the corner. The intersecting casing has to be ripped to the proper width, but now it butts against the solid wood strip instead of slipping behind the other casing. When casings come too close together on the same wall, add a strip between the neighboring casings to make the trim continuous When it comes time to paint, you'll be patting yourself on the back.

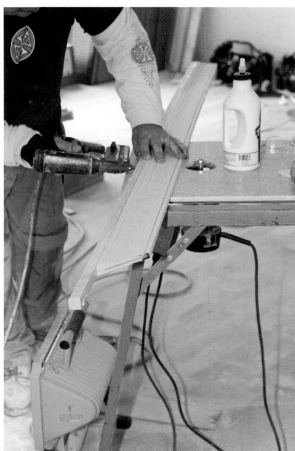

Where there is a small gap left between adjacent door casings on the same wall, fill in the gap with a narrow strip of wood (above).

When a door casing abuts another casing on an adjacent wall in a hallway, sometimes it's best to glue and nail a strip of wood along the edge of the casing to build it out (top left). The abutting casing is then ripped to fit against the strip, creating a cleaner and easier-to-finish joint (left).

Kitchen Cabinets and Bathroom Vanities

One of the biggest steps in finishing your house is to install the kitchen cabinets. The kitchen is usually the heart of a home, and putting in kitchen cabinets goes a long way toward your house becoming a home. I'm going to assume that you ordered your cabinets from either a home center or a kitchen company as opposed to making your own. Although I would never discourage someone from making their own cabinets, manufactured cabinets have come a long way. And because the finishes are applied in a factory environment, they tend to be more uniform and generally superior to finishes you can apply on site.

If you've survived the ordering process, you know that the choices in cabinets can be daunting. In addition to the materials that the cabinets themselves are made of, there seems to be endless choices for the finished look: inset versus overlay doors and drawers, solid doors versus raised-panel doors versus flat-panel doors versus beaded-panel doors, and so on. And drawers can have the same choices, plus choices in drawer slides and pulls. Then there are all the custom, specific-use cabinets—and we haven't even mentioned color or type of wood. In addition, you'll need to pick out the countertops. Oh, and don't forget to order the bathroom vanities while you're at it. You know, building your own cabinets just might be a less stressful way to go.

Base Cabinets First

If you've never been on site when a kitchen order is delivered, be forewarned. It always looks as though there are many more cabinets than you possibly could have ordered, especially if there are bathroom vanities mixed in with the delivery. Before the truck arrives, make sure that the kitchen area is as clean and as free of tools and debris as possible. Once the area is full of "boxes" (that's what they call the cabinets before they're installed), cleanup and preparation can be problematic, if not impossible. Try to be there for the

How does all this become a kitchen? When the cabinet order is delivered, place the cabinets as close to the kitchen space as possible to minimize having to move the cabinets. Also check carefully to make sure the order is complete.

SHOULD I TACKLE THIS MYSELF?

Pros

Like most of the finish carpentry tasks in a house, installing cabinets is not something that should intimidate a person with good basic finish carpentry skills. Cabinets usually go in fairly quickly and easily, and the biggest challenge is keeping everything level and in a line.

Cons

The biggest reason for not installing the cabinets yourself is a warranty issue if the kitchen company doesn't do the installation. Another reason would be time. Even though installation generally goes pretty quickly, it might make sense to have a pro take on the job if you have other deadlines looming or if you're knee-deep in other finishing tasks.

ESTIMATING MATERIALS

Estimating is really not a factor with a kitchen. The kitchen plan should detail every piece of material needed for the kitchen, including filler strips, cabinet end covers, and any decorative molding. When ordering the kitchen, make sure every one of these details has been accounted for. Kitchens routinely take six weeks to eight weeks for delivery. If you leave a small, seemingly insignificant piece out of your order, getting that piece in could delay finishing the kitchen by weeks.

Working off the kitchen plan, place the cabinets close to their final installation spots and remove the protective packaging.

Before the installation begins, do a rough check for level along all walls. This check will alert you to any major discrepancies that might have to be addressed.

delivery. Give each box a quick check for any obvious damage. They are usually wrapped in protective packaging, and torn packaging could indicate damage underneath. Also, have your order sheet and kitchen plan in hand to check off the pieces as they come in. Now is the time to make sure your order is complete, and to catch anything that might not be exactly what you ordered.

Sort the cabinets first

With most of the houses I worked on over the years, extra space was not a luxury. I always tried to have the delivery folks put the cabinets as close to the kitchen as possible, which usually meant putting them in the kitchen. Sorting the cabinets may take a little longer, but at least you don't need to carry them from a remote location. I don't like to handle heavy, bulky items more than once if it's not necessary. And doing so increases the chance of damaging the cabinets in the process.

Start by setting the base cabinets roughly where they will be going. Unwrap them as you go. You'll probably end up with quite a lot of packaging, so pile it neatly or it will be in your way. At this point you are doing more of an organizational placement than beginning the actual installation. If there is an island, unwrap and place those cabinets in their rough position as well. Move all the wall cabinets as well as the vanities out of your way for now. On this project, a nearby pantry closet became temporary housing for the cabinets in waiting.

While the cabinets are in their relative position on the floor, get a rough idea of how level they are in relation to each other. Use the longest level that you own, and if you don't have a long level that's dependable, use a shorter, more dependable level on top of the long level. The aim here is to span as many cabinets as possible for overall accuracy. Check the level in both directions. Look for any "trends" in the level. The floors in a new home are usually pretty level, but even small discrepancies can become compounded as you work along a wall. The rule of thumb is to start at the highest point and shim the rest of the cabinets to that level. The alternative is cutting down the bottom of each cabinet until it's level with the rest.

Align the centered cabinets first

In most kitchens, the cabinets that guide the installation are centered on certain spaces. Those centered cabinets should be indicated on the kitchen plan. By

the way, your kitchen plan should have all the dimensions of the cabinets plus exact figures for their placement. The plan also has measurements from adjacent walls for positioning any island cabinets. Windows are the most common place to center a cabinet, either under a window or between two windows.

To align the cabinet between two windows, measure the distance between the window casings and divide by two. Mark that distance on the wall and write a "CL" over the line to indicate that it is the centerline

The Kitchen Plan

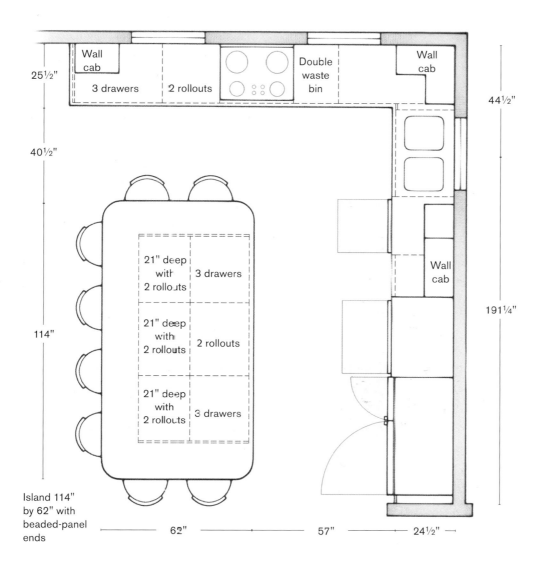

The key cabinets are centered either between two windows or under a window. Measure and mark the centerline for both the space and the cabinet below.

Place a doubled shingle at each stud location and drive a long screw through a predrilled hole.

of the space. Measure and mark the centerline of the base cabinet that is centered between the windows. Slide the cabinet against the wall and align the two centerline marks. Mark the sides of the cabinet near the top to help to guide the side-to-side placement of the adjacent cabinets. Also at this point mark the stud locations just above the top line of the base cabinets.

Three-way alignment

You now have the side-to-side positions marked for three of the base cabinets on the first wall: the center cabinet and the cabinets on either side. Start with the cabinet on the uphill side (if there is one). Using shims 1 in. to $1\frac{1}{2}$ in. wide, level the cabinet front-to-back as well as side-to-side. At one of the studs, place a doubled shim between the back of the cabinet and the wall to create about a $\frac{1}{2}$-in. space. This space allows you to move the rest of the cabinets in or out to keep them in a perfectly straight line as you encounter variations in the wall. The space also makes it easier to scribe the end cabinet to the wall. And anchoring the cabinet at one point allows the cabinet to pivot slightly at that point if need be.

With the first two cabinets aligned and level, place double shims behind the cabinet at each stud. Drive a 3-in. screw through the back of the cabinet, through the shims, and into the wall framing. Snug the next cabinet in place, again shimming the bottom of the free side until it's level in both directions. Again place a double shim behind the cabinet at the stud, and anchor the cabinet in place with a screw. Use a

Predrilling Holes

You may be tempted to just drive your screws right through the back of the cabinet and into the wall, but it's not a good idea. Always predrill through the cabinet and the shims for the screw. The hole keeps the shims from splitting as the screw passes through them, and it also allows the screw to pull the cabinet tight against the wall.

Shim Sharing

If you've gotten your cabinets from a reputable company, they should be completely uniform in height and depth. One trick to streamline the installation process is to share shims. At the front of the cabinet, a shim can support and align the corners of two adjacent cabinets. Similarly in the back, one shim can support and align two cabinets. If the sides of the cabinets are identical, the shared shims should work to level both cabinets. At that point it's just a matter of shimming the "free" side of the second cabinet to make it level.

Shared shims can level and align two cabinets at once. Place the shim so that it supports the sides of adjacent cabinets in the front (above) and in the back (right).

With one side leveled automatically by the shared shims, it's just a matter of bringing the other side of the cabinet up to the same level.

As you work along the line of cabinets, use a straightedge to make sure the face frames of the cabinet are in a perfect line.

straightedge to align the fronts of the cabinets, but don't attach the cabinets together yet.

Scribe the end cabinet to the wall

Up to this point the sides of the cabinets are hidden by the adjacent cabinet. But the end cabinet doesn't have that luxury. The exposed panel on the end cabinet is extra deep so that it can be scribed to fit against the wall precisely. To scribe the panel, first level the cabinet front-to-back next to its neighbor with the end panel almost touching the wall. Make sure the top back edge of the cabinet is perfectly parallel to the wall. Set your compass scribes to the distance between the face of the end cabinet and the face of the adjacent cabinet. Now draw the scribe line, allowing the point of the scribes to ride along the wall. It's important to keep the point and the pencil of the scribes in a perfectly level line as you mark down the end panel. Otherwise the pencil will not record a line perfectly parallel to the wall.

End cabinets have a wider side panel so they can be scribed to fit against the wall. To set up the scribe, first shim the cabinet level (right). Then set compass scribes to the distance that the cabinet needs to go back to be even with its neighbor (far right). Make your scribe line with the compass point riding along the wall.

Make the initial cut close to the line with a circular saw, and then fine-tune to the scribe line with a belt sander. As you cut to the line, add a slight back bevel to ensure a tight fit. Set the cabinet in place and shim it level in both directions. Shim and anchor the back of the end cabinet to the wall at a stud as you did with the cabinets before. Align the front face of the end cabinet with its neighbor and clamp the adjacent sides together. Then predrill a countersunk hole and drive a 1¼-in. screw to join the sides. Double-check to make sure that all the cabinet faces are still in line and that the tops of the cabinets are level, and join the sides of the rest of the base cabinets. Finally, go back and trim the shims even with the tops of the cabinets.

Make the initial cut close to the scribe line with a circular saw (far left), then fine-tune to the line with a belt sander (left).

Double-check the alignment of the cabinet faces. Then clamp the sides together and drive a countersunk screw to fasten them together permanently.

Place the end cabinet in position and then level it in both directions.

When the cabinets are level and fastened together, go back and trim the shims flush with the tops of the cabinets.

The corner cabinet screws to the wall to complete the base cabinets along that wall.

On the opposite wall, the sink base is centered below the window. To find the centerline of the window, measure from the outside of the side casings.

Base cabinets on the adjacent wall

The corner cabinet completes the run of cabinets along the first wall and attaches to the wall the same as the other cabinets. The first cabinet on the adjacent wall is the sink cabinet. In most American kitchens, the sink is centered under the window. Not sure why, but when I was a kid, looking out the window made me forget that I had to do the dishes. This kitchen followed that tradition and the sink base was the first cabinet to go in. With the first cabinet on the other wall, we found the centerline between the windows. This time we find the actual centerline of the window by measuring the casing from outside to outside. That mark is made on the sill, or in this case on the drywall below the sill.

Because of the plumbing, it's a little more complicated to center the sink base cabinet on the window. The plumbing prevents the cabinet from sliding back against the wall, and holes have to be drilled to accommodate the plumbing. To center the cabinet, start by marking the centerline on both the front and the back edges. Then slide the cabinet as close to the wall as possible, in this case, against the supply plumbing. Align a straightedge (a level will work fine) with both marks on the cabinet and extend it back until it reaches the centerline mark on the wall. Measure from the back of the cabinet to the wall at both sides to make sure that the back of the cabinet is

The plumbing pipes prevent the sink base from sliding against the wall. To align the cabinet, make centerline marks on the front and back edges, and then use a straightedge to line them up with the centerline of the window.

perfectly parallel with the wall. The cabinet is now centered, and the plumbing locations can be marked on the back of the cabinet with a pencil.

The holes for the supply plumbing have to be drilled through the floor of the cabinet. The marks show the side-to-side location of the pipes, so tip the cabinet forward and with a square sitting against the back bottom edge of the cabinet, measure down and mark the distance that the pipes are from the wall. With an oversize spade bit chucked into a drill, start both holes until the point of the bit comes through the inside. Now drill from the inside to make perfect holes with no tearout. For the larger exit-plumbing hole, find the center of the pipe on the back of the cabinet. Drill

through at that mark with the pilot drill from a hole saw. Cut a little ways through with the hole saw and then finish the cut from the inside as you did with the supply holes. The final cutout is for the electrical supply for the dishwasher and garbage disposal. When all the holes are cut, lift the cabinet up and slip it carefully over the supply pipes. There should be enough play in the holes to align the cabinet and attach it in place.

With the sink base centered on the window, there was still a gap between the left side of the cabinet and the corner cabinet on the other wall. Spacer blocks supplied by the cabinet manufacturer are ripped to fit between the side of the sink base and the corner

For the exit plumbing, drill from your location in the back with a hole saw. Then complete the hole from inside the cabinet.

With the cabinet in position, reach behind and mark the position of the exit plumbing pipe as well as the side-to-side positions of the supply pipes.

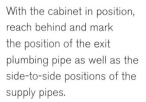

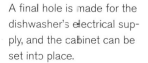

A final hole is made for the dishwasher's electrical supply, and the cabinet can be set into place.

After shimming and leveling the cabinet, rip blocks to fill in the space to the corner cabinet. Put in a block along the top edges (right), as well as the face frames (below).

cabinet, as well as between the face frame and the corner cabinet. The extra space makes the cabinets easier to install and also ensures that the door and drawers on the adjacent corner cabinets don't interfere with each other. As before, the cabinet is leveled across from the corner cabinet as well as front-to-back with shims. When the cabinet position is set, insert shims at the stud locations and anchor the cabinet with 3-in. screws.

Leave room for the dishwasher

Just when you thought it was safe to go ahead and screw all the cabinets together, along comes the dishwasher, the most common under-the-counter appliance. Other such appliances include under-counter refrigerators, ice makers, trash compactors, and wine coolers. These appliances slide into place below the countertop, so a space has to be left for them between the cabinets. The dimensions of these spaces are spelled out precisely in the appliance manufacturer's specifications. So the first step is measuring over the specified distance to position the cabinet on the other side of the dishwasher.

The sink base is then screwed to the wall at the stud locations.

Just as with the other run of base cabinets, the faces of these cabinets need to be perfectly in line. Set a straightedge against the cabinets so that it bridges the dishwasher opening. Place a level on a straightedge and level the cabinet across the dishwasher space at both the front and the back. When the cabinet is set in all three directions, shim the back at the stud locations and secure the cabinet with 3-in. screws.

Next in line in this kitchen is a tall oven cabinet, which is deeper than the base cabinets so that the countertop can terminate against its side. A wall cabinet as well as the base cabinet attach directly to the oven cabinet. Like the end cabinet on the other wall, this tall cabinet comes with extra-deep sides for scribing to the wall if necessary. Only a short section of the back edge between the base cabinet and wall cabinet is exposed, so the top-to-bottom fit is not as crucial as it was with the end cabinet on the other wall. Using a circular saw, rip the sides of the cabinet to the specified depth. The cabinet covers most of the wall, so before you set the cabinet in place, locate the studs and then mark and drill holes at their locations inside the cabinet. Now when you put the cabinet in position there's no guesswork in finding the studs. Set the cabinet in place and make sure that both the front and the side are plumb. Drive screws at the stud holes and also into the side of the adjacent base cabinet to hold it in position.

Make sure that the cabinets on either side of the dishwasher are level both in the back (top) and the front (above). The cabinet can then be screwed to the wall.

Use a straightedge to make sure the faces of the cabinets align on both sides of the dishwasher.

Next in line is a tall cabinet that will house the oven. After scribing the sides of the cabinet to the wall, plumb the sides and front and screw it to the studs.

Build the Island

You may have noticed from the photos that the island was taking shape at the same time that the base cabinets were going in. While one of the crewmembers worked on the base cabinets along the wall, a second crewmember put the island together.

Measure off the walls

The island goes together like the base cabinets along the wall, except that they are freestanding with no wall to anchor to. When I installed island cabinets as a contractor, I'd attach nailer blocks to the floor to keep the cabinets firmly in place. But those blocks always interfered with the shims, and getting the blocks precisely where I needed them was a frustrating experience at best. I asked this crew about that practice, and they said they almost never use nailing blocks. Instead they rely mostly on the sheer size and weight of the island as a unit, along with the heavy slab of granite countertop, to keep the island in place.

As the boxes were unwrapped, they were put in order and placed roughly where they would be going. For the island, start by screwing the first three cabinets together. Remove the doors and drawers and clamp the cabinets together with the face frames in perfect alignment. Drive four screws through the sides, two in front and two in back, to join the cabinets together. When all three cabinets are together, measure off the wall at both ends to get them in their exact position. Using shims and a flat bar to do the lifting, level the three cabinet units lengthwise as well as front to back. Make sure that the backs of each cabinet are shimmed level as well. Double-check the measurement from the wall and, when you're satisfied, mark the position of the cabinets on the floor as a reference while you build the other side of the island.

Start building the island by screwing the sides of the cabinets together. Clamps hold the sides together while you drive the screws.

With the cabinets joined together, measure off the wall at both ends to set their position.

Shim and level the group of cabinets across the front, as well as along the sides. A flat bar gently lifts the cabinet as the shims are inserted.

The other half of this island is made of three cabinets as well, but the outside cabinets are wider than their counterparts on the first side. Begin by installing the middle cabinet. Line up the edges of the cabinet with its neighbor on the opposite side of the island. Then level across from the other side and shim the cabinet accordingly. Level the front of the cabinet as well, and drive screws through the back of the cabinet to anchor it in place. The other two cabinets go in using the same techniques of leveling and attaching. When the cabinets are shimmed and level, clamp and screw the face frames together, keeping them perfectly flush.

The last step to building this island was cutting and fitting V-groove end panels. The voids left by the narrower cabinets created a place for electrical outlets at either end of the island without having wires inside the cabinet. First, filler pieces were ripped to extend the face frames of the narrow cabinets. Then the end panels were set in place with cutouts made for the kickspace at the bottom corners. The panels were then clamped and screwed to the island cabinets, and corner cleats were used to attach the panels to the filler.

Wall Cabinets Next

No project is ever simple, and the wall cabinets in this project brought out a unique challenge. They had to fit under the soffit, but the soffit wasn't perfectly level or even. With a little head scratching, the crew figured out a strategy to make the wall cabinets look even while leaving ample room for trim to finish off the tops of the cabinets.

Start in the corner

The corner wall cabinet is the first one to go in. In this case it had windows on either side, so there were no adjacent cabinets to worry about. First, a measurement was made from the soffit and a level line was drawn on both walls for the bottom of the cabinet. The wire for

After attaching the center cabinet to its back-to-back neighbor, level the cabinets in place on either side (top). Clamp and screw the face frames together (above) and then drive screws to join both sides of the island together.

The extra spaces at the ends of the island were for electrical outlets. A filler piece spanned the gap and then a V-groove end panel covered the entire end of the island. A corner cleat securely joined the end panel to the filler piece.

the under-cabinet lighting was brought down to just below the level line, per the electrician's instructions. The studs were located and their locations written down. Like most carpentry projects, prep work is sometimes the most time-consuming part, but it saves headaches and sore backs in the long run, especially when hanging wall cabinets. Armed with the stud locations, begin prepping the cabinet by removing the doors. Then measure over and mark the stud locations inside the cabinet and drill holes at each location near the top. Before lifting the cabinet into place, start screws in each of the holes you drilled.

Make sure your level is within easy reach and that your driver drill is ready and waiting inside the cabinet. Set the cabinet on top of a wooden prop (see the sidebar at right) and hold it against the wall with one hand. With the other hand, grab the level and

check the side of the cabinet for plumb. When you're satisfied, grab your driver drill and drive the screws that you started in the holes. Now check the face frame for plumb. Shim out at the studs along the bottom edge if necessary and drive screws to secure the bottom of the cabinet.

The next cabinet to install is centered between the windows above our first base cabinet. Like the cabinet below, locate and mark the centerlines on both the

Plumb the sides of the cabinet and then drive the screws into the studs to hold the cabinet in place.

TIP

A Short Piece of Wood Gives the Wall Cabinets a Leg Up

When you go to hang a wall cabinet, you always seem to be short on hands as you hold the cabinet in place and attach it to the wall. A simple piece of wood that goes from the top of the base cabinet to the level line gives you something to rest the wall cabinet on while you attach it to the wall.

Cut a short piece of wood to go between the top of the base cabinet and the level line. The piece of wood acts as a prop so that the cabinet can be installed by one person.

wall and the cabinet. Then measure from the center-line and mark the stud locations. As with the corner cabinet, drill holes for screws at the stud locations. Draw a level line on the wall for the bottom of the cabinet. This cabinet is shorter in height, so it gets mounted higher. With the higher cabinet, it's more difficult to hold it in place and drive the screws, so have another crewmember hold the cabinet on the level line while you drive the screws to secure the cabinet. The wall cabinet at the end of that wall is also a stand-alone unit, so the entire installation procedure is the same. This time the cabinet was positioned the same distance from the window casing as the middle wall cabinet for a symmetrical look. Like the corner cabinet, the end cabinet was taller, so attaching it to the wall was a one-person job with the help of the wooden prop.

On the adjacent wall, two wall cabinets join together to fit in the space next to the tall oven cabinet. It's easiest to put these cabinets up as a single unit, so clamp and screw them together before they go up. The installation procedure was then the same as before with the wooden prop. The only difference is that the right side of the wall cabinets screwed into the side of the oven cabinet.

Two cabinets join together to make the wall unit for the adjacent wall. Before they go into place, clamp and screw the two cabinets together (left). Then, using the wooden prop, set the cabinets in place and screw them to the wall (below).

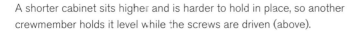
A shorter cabinet sits higher and is harder to hold in place, so another crewmember holds it level while the screws are driven (above).

Factory-made trim is custom ripped to fit between the tops of the cabinets and the soffit. Inside corners are simple butt joints, whereas outside corners are mitered.

TIP

A Small Overhang Makes the Cleanest Joint

When adding a filler strip such as the trim between the soffit and the top of the cabinet, it's next to impossible to make a flush seam that appears seamless. Instead, the crew on this job let the trim overhang the edge of the cabinet by about ¼ in., which creates a shadow line and eliminates the need for a perfect joint.

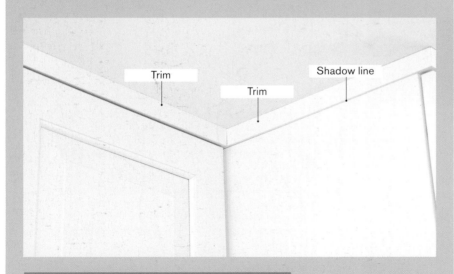

Trim   Trim   Shadow line

A slight overhang means the joint between the trim and the cabinet doesn't have to be perfect, and it creates a shadow line for visual interest as well.

The only thing left is to install trim to fill the gap between the top of the cabinet and the soffit. Because of the irregularity of the soffit, the width of the gap was inconsistent and each piece had to be custom ripped to the proper size. Outside corners of the trim were mitered at 45 degrees and inside corners were simple butt joints.

Bathroom Vanities

Compared to kitchen cabinets, bathroom vanities are simple and straightforward to install. Most often, vanities are basically stand-alone sink-base cabinets, although cabinets can be combined to create just about any design you want. Cabinet combinations are installed much like those in a kitchen. For our purposes, the vanity is a simple, single-cabinet installation.

Templating for Countertops

When the cabinets are installed, call the countertop people immediately. It often takes weeks for the countertops to be ready. Again, the choices in countertop materials can be overwhelming, and most require special tools and skills to create and install. From stone to laminates and synthetics, I'd leave this step to the pros for the best-looking results.

Although I don't recommend making your own countertops, templating can be a valuable skill to learn. If you've never watched a pro make a template for a countertop, be sure to be on hand for it. The process is fascinating and can be used in many different applications in carpentry. Strips of ¼-in. plywood are set in place to delineate the exact area of the countertop. These strips can be scribed to irregularities in the walls or other mating surfaces if necessary. The strips are hot-glued and stapled together. Numerous indexing points and reference notes are made, such as the sink centerline, to guide the fabricators who transfer the templated shape to the countertop material.

With the cabinet installation complete, the countertop professionals can make templates for the countertops. The templates are deceptively simple: strips of ¼-in. plywood that delineate the edges of all the countertops. The strips are hot-glued and stapled together.

Vanity placement

Like the kitchen cabinets, the exact placement of the vanity is usually spelled out on the plans. If the vanity happens to be on a wall all by itself, just go by the measurements on the plan. A more common scenario is the vanity placed next to the toilet and often there are other issues, such as the door into the bathroom or the shower door, to consider. The vanity should not interfere with any of these things. The vanity described here sits between the toilet and the bathroom door. The plumbing code specifies minimum distance on either side of the toilet (15-in. minimum from the center of the flange to the walls or vanity on both sides), so the toilet becomes the crucial item for placement. By the way, if you believe that the flange is too close to the wall, or if insufficient room was left next to the proposed placement of the vanity, get the plumber and/or the building official to sign off on the discrepancy or suggest a solution.

This particular bathroom had plenty of room for the toilet to fit next to the vanity with symmetrical space on either side of the tank. Measure from the wall to the center of the toilet flange and double that measurement, which is the distance that the vanity needs to sit from the wall. Like the sink base in the kitchen, you'll need to cut holes in the back of the vanity to accommodate the plumbing. In this case, both supply and exit plumbing come from the wall. Slide the vanity up to the plumbing stubs and measure the placement distance from the wall beside the toilet. Also measure to make sure the back of the vanity is parallel with the wall. Reach down behind the vanity and mark the position of the pipes on the back of the vanity. Now drill the holes for the plumbing (see the sidebar on pp. 152–153).

With the holes drilled, slide the vanity into place and position it precisely from the wall.

Level and install the vanity

Slide the vanity all the way to the wall and take a
precise measurement from the wall on the other side
of the toilet. Make the measurement at both the front
and back of the vanity to make sure that there isn't a
discrepancy. The installation now is the same as for a
kitchen base cabinet. Shim the vanity level both
front-to-back and side-to-side. Then shim behind the
back edge of the vanity as needed at each stud location
and drive 3-in. screws, making sure to predrill each
hole first. The final step is trimming the shims with a
utility knife, and the installation is done.

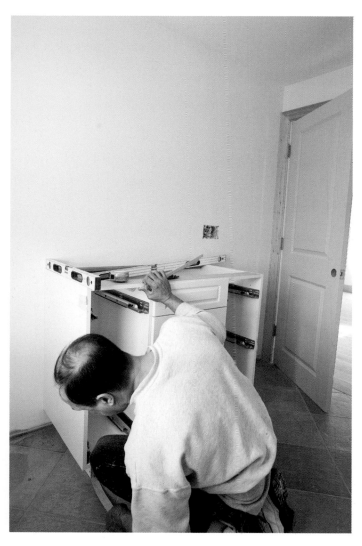

Shim the vanity level in both directions (left),
and then screw through the back of the vanity
and into the studs to hold it in place (above).
The last step in the installation is cutting the
shims off with a utility knife.

Perfect Plumbing Holes

If you've ever tried to drill a clearance hole for a pipe in one shot, you probably experienced tearout or blowout of the material where the drill bit exited. The bit or hole saw also has a tendency to bind in the hole, which can wrench your wrist if you're not careful. Avoiding the problem is easy.

The bigger holes for the exit plumbing should be cut with a hole saw, which has a circular blade with a pilot or guide bit in the center. Start from your location mark on the back side of the vanity and drill in with the pilot bit. Let the hole saw cut into the material about 1/8 in. Now move inside the vanity, insert the pilot bit into the guide hole, and complete the cut. Your first cut scored the material from the back side, so you should have no tearout.

Holes for the supply plumbing are usually cut with a spade bit, which has flat wings that do the cutting with a tapered point as a guide in the middle. Again, start your holes from your marks on the back side, allowing the wings to cut into the material about 1/8 in. Make sure you cut deep enough for the guide point to come all the way through to the inside. Then go inside the vanity, place the point of the bit in the holes just made by the guide point, and drill back through to complete the holes. Again, the holes should be perfect with no tearout and without sprained wrists.

To make perfect holes with a hole saw with no tearout, first drill from the back, cutting into the material slightly with the saw (left). Then, from inside the vanity, insert the pilot bit into the hole and finish the cut (above).

To make smaller holes for the supply plumbing, use a spade bit with a tapered point. Start the hole from your location on the back and cut slightly into the material (right). Then go inside the vanity and stick the guide point into the hole you made from the other side to finish cutting the holes (below).

Stair Trim

One of the wonderful perks of writing about houses and home building is the excitement of learning a new technique or a new approach to a problem. That was the case when I watched master finish carpenter Billy McGraw finish the stairs on this project. I thought I'd seen (and tried) just about every method you can imagine. Billy's technique and approach to the problem were simple and elegant, and he was able to execute the stair finish quickly and efficiently. The staircase was a basic straight run that landed on a bottom platform, with no balusters or newels. The stairs had natural oak treads and painted risers.

Let the Skirt Boards Do the Math

I was all ready for Billy to drop the skirt boards in the spaces next to the stair stringers and to begin running the treads and risers. So I was a bit taken aback to see him leveling over and measuring as if building the stairs from scratch. When I asked him what he was doing, he grabbed his tape measure and showed me discrepancies of almost ½ in. from tread to tread. He smiled and said, "That's why they call it rough framing."

Before indicting the framers, we needed to stop and realize that it had been over three months since the 2×12 stair stringers had been cut and installed on a cold, wet November day, and that they had been exposed to the elements for weeks before the house was weathered in. Then, for the past six weeks, they had been part of the house's heated interior environment. Much of the variation can be attributed directly to the shrinkage of the stringer material. On top of that, most framers cut stringers with circular saws, which are just not accurate enough for finish work.

Lay out and cut the skirt boards

Just as you did at the framing stage, determine the overall rise of the stair, but this time simply divide that figure by the number of rises in the rough-framed stair. This stair was complicated by the platform landing that acts as the first step up from the first floor. Measure down to the landing, but keep in mind that the landing will be covered with ¾-in.-thick oak flooring. To lay out the skirt board, attach stair gauges to a framing square at the rise and run figures, just as

Pros

Finishing stairs can be one of the most challenging but also the most satisfying parts of carpentry. If you enjoyed geometry in school, stair finishing will get your juices flowing as you deal with the stair angles as well as the precise intersection of multiple surfaces.

Cons

Stair finishing is the graduate studies of finish carpentry. I would not recommend you tackle the task unless you are experienced and very confident in your abilities. If you have a carpentry mentor that you work with to help walk you through some of the tougher areas, this would be a good time to bring that person in. Watch and learn!

To estimate materials for finishing a stairway, make a list component by component: skirt boards, risers, treads, scotia, handrail and brackets, etc. Be sure to order treads that give you plenty of length to work with, and order any special treads, such as those with returned ends. In addition, make sure you have plenty of construction adhesive and carpenter's wood glue.

Stair Stringer Shrinkage

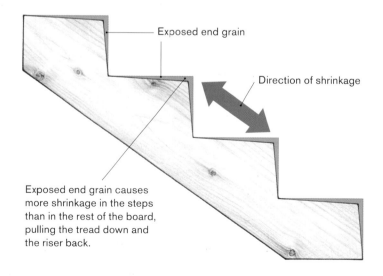

Exposed end grain

Direction of shrinkage

Exposed end grain causes more shrinkage in the steps than in the rest of the board, pulling the tread down and the riser back.

As with the stair stringers, attach stops to a framing square at the rise and run dimensions and lay out the steps on the skirt boards.

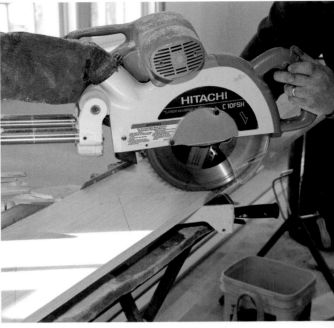

The riser cuts will be exposed, so make them with a miter saw with a finish blade (above). The tread cuts will be hidden and can be made with a jigsaw (below).

you did when laying out the stringers. Mark off the rise and run along the edge of the skirt board. When laying out and cutting the stair stringers, the top and bottom details had to be worked out so the stringers would fit into place. With the skirt boards, you can leave the top end uncut for now and just extend the lines for the floor at the top as well as for the landing over to the edge of the board.

When framing, a carpenter's pencil sharpened with a utility knife to a wide flat "point" is sufficiently accurate for cutting stringers with a circular saw. But because the skirt boards dictate the precise position of the risers and treads, do the layout with a conventional round pencil sharpened to a fine point. With this method the risers tuck behind the skirt boards, making those edges of the skirt visible, so use a sliding compound miter saw with a fine finish blade to give you clean, accurate cuts at every riser line. By the way, your laser-guided miter saw makes quick work of setting the blade to the exact angle of the risers. Use a jigsaw to finish the riser cuts and to cut the tread lines.

Set the first skirt board in place to make sure it fits properly. At this point the top of the skirt should be sitting on top of the oak flooring (without the nosing piece). Set the bottom of the skirt on a scrap of flooring to represent the finished flooring on the

The skirt board has to be notched around the flooring at the top of the stairs, so after adjusting the position of the skirt in relation to the risers, scribe the notch at the top of the stairs.

landing. Now slide the skirt laterally toward the stairs, leaving enough space for risers to slide comfortably between the stringer and the skirt, or about an inch (don't worry, shims will push the risers tight to the skirt board). The nosing at the top of the stairs fits *between* the skirt boards, so the skirts need to be notched to sit on the subfloor as well as the installed floor. When the skirt is in position for the risers, use another scrap of flooring to scribe the notch to fit around the flooring.

First skirt board becomes a template

Before cutting out the notch for the flooring, clamp the first skirt board to the stock for the second, aligning the top edges flush. Carefully trace the shape of the first skirt board onto the second. As with the first skirt board, cut the riser lines with the miter saw for crisp, accurate edges. Now cut the notch for the flooring and the first skirt board should drop into place.

The final cuts on the first skirt board are where it intersects with the baseboard at the top and bottom. There are many different ways to intersect the two trim elements where they change angle; this crew used miter cuts. First they determined that the angle of the stair was 38 degrees. Half of that angle is then 19 degrees.

When the first skirt board is cut and fit satisfactorily, use it as a template to mark and cut the rises and runs of the second skirt.

Set your miter saw and make a 19-degree angle cut on the end of a baseboard scrap. With the skirt board in position, slide the scrap of baseboard over until the long point hits the upper edge of the skirt. Trace along the edge of the scrap for the cut line. At the bottom of the skirt, set the scrap of baseboard on a piece of flooring. This time, let the short point of the cut intersect with the upper edge of the skirt and trace your cut line. Now just cut to those lines and make slots for biscuits in each end.

Before installing the skirt board permanently, mark the top and bottom of the skirt and snap a line to make sure the skirt goes in perfectly straight. Apply a liberal amount of construction adhesive to the back side of the skirt, and with two crewmembers—one at the top and one at the bottom—slip the skirt into place, taking care not to smear the adhesive on the drywall. Align the top edge of the skirt board with the snapped line and nail the skirt at the top and bottom with 2½-in. finish nails. By the way, this is one of those times to have the phone number of the framer on speed-dial. Call him up and thank him for installing blocking along the stair for the skirt boards (see the top left photo on p. 15). Otherwise you'd have to hunt for every stud in the wall.

To scribe the top of the skirt to the baseboard, cut the miter angle on a baseboard scrap and slide it over until the two top edges meet. Draw a line along the edge for the cut.

Snap a chalkline to make sure that the skirt board goes in perfectly straight. Then install the skirt, adjusting it to follow the line as you go.

Risers help position the other skirt board

The first skirt board is installed exactly where it needs to be to finish the stairs. Now you need to get the second skirt board perfectly in line with the first. The way to do that is by temporarily installing three risers, one at the top, one at the bottom, and one in the middle. Start by ripping riser stock to whatever measurement you cut on the skirts—in this case 7⁄8 in. wide. Cut the length of the risers to the width of the stair chase minus 7⁄8 in. The riser needs to slide in behind the skirt on one side and then clear the other

skirt before it slides in on that side. Set the first riser in place one step up from the bottom and level it across, shimming it if need be. When the riser is level, tack it to the stringer. Repeat that process for a riser near the middle of the stairs and then again one step down from the top.

Set the second skirt on top of the risers, and it should be perfectly level in relation to the first skirt. As with the first skirt, you need to notch it for the finished flooring at the top of the stair, so slip a flooring scrap over the first riser to lift the skirt an equal amount. Slide the skirt in or out until the gap between the skirt

To get the second skirt board installed at the right height, temporarily install three risers: one at the top, one in the middle, and one at the bottom. Level each one and tack it to the stringers.

Set the second skirt on top of the three risers to test the fit. A scrap of flooring lifts the bottom of the skirt, so the top can be scribed around the flooring.

At the bottom of the stair, mark the line where the skirt board crosses the inside wall. That line is the short point of a 45-degree cut to wrap the trim around the stub wall.

board and the stringer is about the same as on the other side. As with the first skirt board, scribe and cut the notch at the top for the flooring and then set the skirt back in place. Make a rough check to see if the skirt board is square to the riser. If it's off by a lot, you may have to adjust the skirt in or out to make it closer. At the top of the stair, trace the baseboard intersection point just as you did on the other side.

The bottom end of the second skirt board is different, as the stairs and skirt wrap around the corner and onto the landing. With the skirt board set in place, draw the line of the wall on the back side of the skirt. To wrap around the corner, cut a 45-degree angle along the line you just traced. The second skirt can then be glued and nailed in place. With both skirts installed, the math and geometry are essentially done for the main run of stairs.

The first risers help to lock the stringers in position. Glue and wedge the ends of each riser against the skirt, then use a straightedge to position the middle of the riser.

ESSENTIAL TECHNIQUE

Making Wedges

The key to installing the risers and treads with the method described here is shimming behind the risers so they butt against the skirts. An ample gap was purposely left for the shims, and you would need a huge pile of conventional shims to fill the space on every step. A better idea is to make your own wedges or shims. Start by making some 3-in.-wide boards with the grain going perpendicular to the length of the board. Stack up two boards, set the saw at about 5 degrees, and saw off one end of the pair. Flip the boards over and cut through from the other side, lining the blade up with the short point. That should give you a pair of wedges or shims about ¾ in. across at their widest. Every time you flip the board and cut through, you should end up with an identical pair. You'll need 6 to 9 wedges per riser, plus others in key places, so make at least 100 of them.

On the other side of the landing, a short section of skirt board is scribed to the flooring. Then the baseboard intersection angles are cut and the mini-skirt is installed.

When both skirts are installed, the riser is wedged over against the skirt. A short section of skirt completes the transition trim on the other side as well.

When the glue has cured on the return riser for the first step, straighten and wedge the riser at the middle stringer.

Landing details

It's always best to start at the bottom of the stairs and work your way up. But the bottom step was actually the landing, which required a lot of small details. Before beginning those details, the crew permanently installed the first three risers to help lock the skirts in position. First, glue was applied between the risers and the skirt, and then wedges were driven between the stringer and the risers to push each riser against the skirt. Finish nails driven through the riser at each wedge hold the assembly in place. After the ends of the riser were secure, the middle was adjusted with wedges until it was straight and then nailed in place.

The landing was complicated by the fact that the wall along the inside edge of the stair stuck out a couple of inches past the intersecting wall, creating a stub wall. The trim would have to wrap around this

detail. The bottom riser on the main stair extended over and returned back to the side of the stub wall. On the other side of the landing a short section of skirt board bridged between the landing baseboard and the first-floor baseboard. It just so happened that the piece cut off from the bottom of the second skirt worked perfectly for this skirt. First, a riser was ripped and set in place for the step up to the landing. The skirt cutoff was set in place, and the thickness of the flooring was traced and scribed off the bottom as before. Then the baseboard intersection lines were traced and cut, along with slots for biscuits. After the short skirt section was glued and nailed in place, the riser was wedged over and nailed. A short section of skirt filled in the other side as well. After attaching the return piece to the bottom riser of the main stair, the riser was wedged, straightened, and glued in place.

The wedges become a permanent part of the stairs, so apply yellow glue to both sides before driving them in.

Drive nails through the riser and into the stringer at each wedge position.

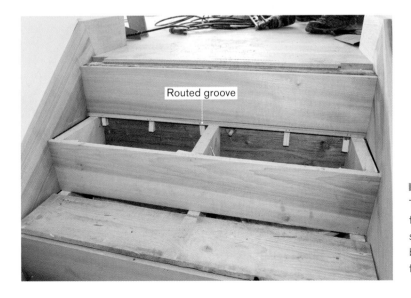

Routed groove

The top riser can't be accessed from behind to attach the tread, so a groove is cut along the bottom edge of the piece where the top tread will fit.

Finish the risers

Now the rest of the risers can be cut and installed. For each riser, first remove the temporary tread from the step above. Put a bead of glue on both ends of the riser and slip it into place behind the skirt boards. As before, spread glue on the wedges and drive them behind the riser to snug it against the skirt board. If a larger gap needs to be filled, drive wedges from both sides of the stringer to fill the gap. It's important to maintain the same routine for every step. Each wedge must be glued as it goes in, and at least two wedges should be driven in at each stringer, one at the top and one at the bottom. If there is any cup in the riser, drive a third wedge in the middle of the riser to push it tight against the skirt. Make sure that a finish nail is driven through the riser at every wedge to hold the assembly together until the glue sets. After the riser is installed, reinstall the temporary treads.

The top riser gets a little different treatment. When it comes time to install the treads, each one attaches to the riser above with screws that are driven through the riser from behind. Because the top riser is against the floor framing, this attachment is impossible. Instead, a groove is routed along the bottom edge of the riser. A matching tongue on the back of the top tread will slip into the groove. The top riser is supported from behind with multiple wedges along its length to keep it perfectly straight.

Before you begin to install the flooring on the landing, complete the baseboard around the landing connecting the main skirt board with the skirt running from the landing to the first floor.

Installing Treads

To install the treads, begin at the bottom of the stairs and work your way up. That means starting with the landing once again. Treat the main area of the landing like a large tread. Every other tread fits between the skirt boards, and for consistency in appearance, the flooring on the landing should butt against the baseboard. (Note that this is the only place in the entire house where this detail is used.) Before you begin the finished floor on the landing, install the baseboard. Recall that we set the baseboard on a scrap of flooring when we marked the intersecting cut on the skirt. In order for the landing baseboard to fit behind the flooring and still be the same height as the rest of the baseboard in the house, it needs to be taller. As you put the baseboard in, level it from the main skirt board over to the corner, and then from there to the skirt board for the landing step. You should now have an uninter-

rupted even line from the second-floor baseboard all the way to the baseboard on the first floor. By the way, the baseboard can be completed at the top of the stair as well at this point.

The tread detail used on this project was a fairly typical installation: 3/4-in.-thick treads with a bullnose edge that extended over the riser 1 1/2 in. A 3/4-in.-wide scotia molding completed the detail from below (see the drawing on p. 164). Again we start with the landing, and the finished surface of the landing begins with the nosing. Because the first riser of the main stair returned around the stub wall, it was convenient to have the back edge of the nosing butt against the riser return. The nosing is ripped from tread stock, so begin by measuring from the return to the edge of the riser below and then add 1 1/2 in. for the overhang. That measurement is the width of rip. Take the nosing stock you just made and cut it to fit exactly across the landing. Spread construction adhesive on the subfloor as well as along the top of the riser, and then nail the nosing into place with 2 1/2-in. finish nails.

Tread to Riser Detail

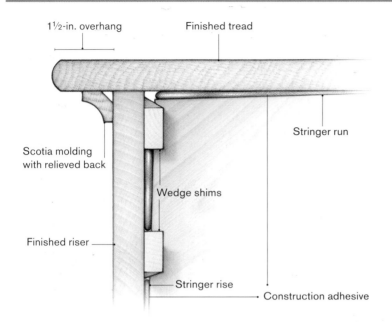

1½-in. overhang

Finished tread

Scotia molding with relieved back

Stringer run

Wedge shims

Finished riser

Stringer rise

Construction adhesive

The landing gets regular flooring

With the nosing installed, the next step is to cover the landing floor. But before the flooring goes down, give the whole area a thorough vacuuming. Any small bit of debris can keep the flooring from sitting flat. The landing gets covered with the same oak-strip flooring as in the rest of the house. Working three strips at a time, copy the exact length and shape using a tread-templating tool (see the sidebar on the facing page). When you've transferred the shape to the strips, set them on the saw as a unit and cut them to the line. This is another time where a laser-guided miter saw earns its keep. With the laser line, you can set the angle of the saw to match your line precisely.

How Tight Should the Treads Fit?

Each tread should fit snugly between the skirts with only "gentle fist" persuasion needed to get it into position. If a tread is too tight, it can spread the skirts and open gaps on the treads you've already installed. Too loose, and joints on the sides of the treads will stick out like a sore thumb. Make your cut to the line, but "leave the line" for a snug fit. If the tread seems too tight, go back to the saw and shave off 1/64 in. at a time until it fits just right.

A laser-guided miter saw makes adjusting the cut to the exact angle of the flooring very quick and easy.

ESSENTIAL TOOL

A Tread-Templating Tool

The angle between the skirt and the riser is almost never exactly 90 degrees. And if one side happens to be exactly square, the other side is usually out of square. So a tread-templating tool is a must. This tool adjusts in length as well as angle to give you a perfect template of each stair tread. Set the tool on the stock and align the back edge of the template with the edge of the stock. Trace along both ends to transfer the shape. And if you're creative, it's not hard to make one of these tools from scratch.

Stair treads are rarely perfectly square, and any variation in the cut can be an eyesore. A stair-templating tool is the perfect solution. Place the tool in the space you wish to template, extending the wings to fit the angle and width (top). Set the template on the stock (in this case flooring for the landing step) and align it with the back edge of the stock (above) Trace the sides for a perfect match of the area templated (above right).

Install the flooring on the landing one strip at a time, gluing it and nailing it through the tongue.

Screw into the flooring from the backside of the bottom riser to lock everything together.

When you've cut the next three strips, spread construction adhesive and install one strip at a time Tap the pieces into place until the strips fit tightly together, and drive finish nails at an angle through the top of the tongue. Continue working across until you get to the other side of the landing. Measure the exact width you need for the final strip and rip it on a tablesaw. Install the last two or three strips as a single unit, tapping them into position with a hammer and a wood block. As we did with the last courses of flooring in each room, face-nail the last three landing courses. Finish the job by screwing the bottom riser to the flooring from the back side of the riser.

The first tread wraps the corner

After the landing, turn to the bottom tread that wraps around the stub wall on top of the returned riser. Start by setting the tread-templating tool between the skirt boards. For this tread, the crew ordered a special tread with a bullnose return on one end. That end is fixed, so it determines the tread layout. Measure the distance from the skirt to the edge of the return. On the tread, mark that measurement from the inside edge of the return nosing, and align the templating tool to that mark. Trace both ends of the tool, letting the line on the left side go just past the stub wall to mark where the tread needs to be cut out. Measure the distance from the back of the tread to the face of the stub wall. Mark that distance on the template line as well as on

the return end of the tread, and connect those marks. Finally, measure and mark the length and width of the return leg of the tread. (Because the inside edge of the return nosing is even with the return riser below, the width of the leg is the return nosing plus ¾ in.)

At the saw, cut the far end of the tread, then cut the notch around the stub wall. The only cuts that will be visible are where the tread joins the skirts and where the return leg meets the wall, so make these cuts with a miter saw. Baseboard will cover the other cuts, so you can make them with a jigsaw and not worry about making super-clean cuts. Tip the jigsaw at a slight angle to back bevel the inside of the return leg. The bevel gives you more room to slide the tread into position.

Test the tread to make sure it's going to fit properly. You don't have to tap it all the way home at this point. Just get it close enough to make sure that the gap along the back edge and the gap between the return leg and

Make the visible cuts for the tread with a miter saw, but cut out for the stub wall with a jigsaw. Tipping the saw creates a back bevel to make the installation easier.

At each step, squirt a healthy bead of construction adhesive between the riser and the stringer before installing the tread.

the wall is the same measurement. Then take the tread back out and apply a generous bead of adhesive on every surface that the tread touches. Also squirt adhesive between the riser and the stringer. Construction adhesive is tenacious stuff, and it strengthens and solidifies the connections. Slide the tread into place at a slight angle to avoid smearing the adhesive. Then tap it down to the stringers and back against the riser. Drive finish nails at each stringer and screws through the riser above and into the back of the tread.

Before continuing up the stairs with treads, it's a good idea to button up the skirt/baseboard details on the landing. As of now, you just have the mitered edge of the left skirt board. It's really difficult and awkward to change more than one direction at a time with any kind of molding, including the base cap molding that finishes the top of the skirt board and baseboard. To help you in this regard, add a small wedge-shaped piece to the top of the skirt so it goes into the wrap-around detail on a level line (see the top photo on p. 168). On the opposite side of the stub wall install a piece of baseboard with a 45-degree mitered edge. Cut a piece of wide stock to go between the miter on the baseboard and the miter on the skirt. Set the piece in place and first draw a level line across the top, even with the top of the skirt. Now mark the height of the baseboard across the piece. Mark a plumb line between the two horizontal lines, allowing plenty of

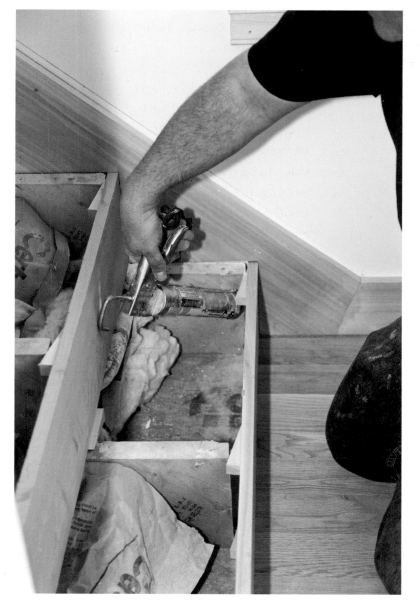

To make the transition of the trim easier as it wraps around the stub wall, a small wedge is added on top of the skirt.

A trim piece on the end of the stub wall transitions from the height of the skirt to the height of the baseboard. First draw horizontal lines across the piece at both heights. Connect the two with a plumb line and then cut out the stepped trim. The base cap can now follow the trim without changing more than one direction at a time.

space for the base cap. This detail may seem busy, but it allows the base cap to follow the trim from the skirt to the baseboard without changing more than one direction at each joint. Make the cuts on the middle piece and then glue and nail it into position.

Installing the rest of the treads

With all the finicky detail work done, installing the regular treads is relatively easy. Just as you did with the risers, develop a routine as you work up the stair. First remove the temporary tread. If you're working by yourself, removing more than one temporary tread at a time probably isn't a big deal, but if there are others working in the house with you, assume that they will need to use the stairs. And you may need to use the stairs as well. More than one tread missing can be a pain as well as downright dangerous.

With the temporary tread removed, set the stair template in place, snugging it against the skirts on the sides and against the riser in the back. After securing all the nuts, carefully lift the template from the stairs and bring it to the saw. Set the tread stock with the back edge against the fence on at least one end. Push the template against the fence at that end and align the other end of the template with the edge of the tread stock. Trace both ends of the template and then cut to the lines.

Again the tread should go into place with very little pressure. A gentle tap with the edge of your hand should be all it needs to drop into place. If it's too tight, go back and shave off just 1/64 in. from one end. Taking off just a little at a time ensures a perfect fit. When you're satisfied with the fit, remove the tread and apply a generous bead of glue on each stringer, as well as a bead along the bottom of the riser in the back and along the top of the riser in the front. And don't forget to squirt adhesive between the stringer and the riser. Now drop the tread back into place, and use a rubber mallet to tap it home against the riser in the back. Nail through the tread at every stringer with three 2½-in. finish nails, and finish off by removing the next temporary tread and driving screws through the back of the riser and into the back edge of the tread (see the photos on p. 170).

Next stop, the top

The treads proceed exactly the same way until you reach the top. At that point you have two challenges: the nosing that continues the flooring and creates the edge of the stair, and the top tread that needs special treatment because the back is inaccessible for screwing. Let's tackle the nosing first. Begin by thoroughly sweeping or vacuuming the subfloor where the nosing will go. Any debris can keep the tread from sitting tight to the floor. Measure the depth of the nosing at both ends. Let the tape measure extend past the riser

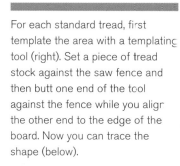

For each standard tread, first template the area with a templating tool (right). Set a piece of tread stock against the saw fence and then butt one end of the tool against the fence while you align the other end to the edge of the board. Now you can trace the shape (below).

To install each tread, first apply a heavy bead of construction adhesive to all mating surfaces (top). Set the tread in place and tap the nosing with a rubber mallet to snug it against the riser (middle). After nailing the tread into the stringers, screw from the back to attach the tread to the riser above (above).

by 1½ in. as we did for the nosing on the landing. In most cases the measurements are the same, and the nosing can simply be ripped on the tablesaw.

Now set your tread template between the skirts for the length of the nosing and cut the nosing as you did the treads. As before, spread a bead of adhesive over all mating surfaces. Press the nosing into place and tap it with a rubber mallet to seat it against the flooring. Drive finish nails along the back edge of the nosing, but hold off on the front edge. Quite often the subfloor at the top of the stairs is worn from the hundreds of boots that have made their way up the stairs during construction. Nailing the nosing to the worn subfloor would make it slant down slightly as it extends over the top riser. Instead, place a bullet level on the flooring and let it extend from the floor onto the nosing. Shim slightly under the nosing until it is perfectly in plane with the flooring. Then drive a finish nail through the nosing at each shim. The construction adhesive on the top edge of the riser should bridge any gap that the shims might create. Finally, trim the shims back to the face of the riser.

Remember back when we did the risers? We gave the top riser a little different treatment, cutting a groove along the bottom edge so that the top tread could slide into it. The top tread needs to have a tongue along the back edge to engage the groove of the riser. First rip the tread stock to your standard tread depth plus ⅜ in. To make the tongue, set up a router with a rabbeting bit equipped with a bearing that makes a ⅜-in.-deep cut. Now set the depth of the cut at ⅜ in. Rout the back edge of the tread to create a ⅜-in. by ⅜-in. tongue. Tip the router slightly to give the tongue a slight taper, making it slide into the groove more easily.

Template the tread as before, but this time set the template in ⅜ in. from the back edge of the stock (to account for the tongue) before tracing the shape. Cutting and installation are the same, except that the groove gets a healthy bead of adhesive along with all the other surfaces. When you slide the tread into place,

When you install the nosing, shim the leading edge up enough to put it in plane with the flooring.

angle the front edge up slightly to align the tongue with the groove. Then tap it home with a rubber mallet and nail it in to the stringers as before. If the tread seems to be bouncing out of the groove as you tap it, measure the overhang to confirm that the tread is in as far as it should go.

Finishing Touches

The treads and risers are in place and now all that's left are the finishing touches. We already installed the base cap on the baseboard, skirt, and transition pieces on the landing; at this point we install the base cap on top of the main skirts and complete the cap to the second-floor baseboard. For long pieces of base cap, it helps to have two crewmembers—one at each end—to hold the piece in place for measuring and marking. Cut all the pieces and make sure they'll fit before gluing and nailing them into place.

The top tread requires a tongue to fit into the groove on the top riser. To create the tongue, put a rabbeting bit in a router with a bearing to make a $3/8$-in.-deep cut. Set the router depth to cut $3/8$ in. as well (left). With the tread upside down, rout along the edge to create the tongue. Keeping the router at a slight angle tapers the tongue for an easier fit (below).

Scotia molding

The next item is the scotia molding that covers the joint between the tread overhang and the riser. Scotia molding is L-shaped and comes with a square back corner. The crew first cut the scotia into rough lengths and then ripped the corner off each length to make the pieces fit more easily. For each piece it was a matter of measuring the length, cutting, and then gluing and nailing the pieces into place. There are a couple of ways to simplify the measuring process (see the sidebar on p. 174). When cutting the pieces, make them slightly long so they spring slightly into place. Then drive brads, alternating one into the riser and the next into the tread to hold the scotia in place until the glue cures.

Install the handrail

The base cap and scotia are purely decorative and just make the stairway look more finished. The last item, the handrail, is a matter of safety as well as code. By code, the handrail has to be a certain distance above the stair nosing and a certain distance away from the

Connect the base cap from the stair skirts to the base cap on the baseboard. Cut all the pieces and fit them together before installing them.

A length of scotia molding finishes off each tread. To make the molding fit more easily, rip the corner off on a tablesaw.

Cut the scotia molding slightly long so it springs into place to create tight end joints.

Attaching the Scotia Molding

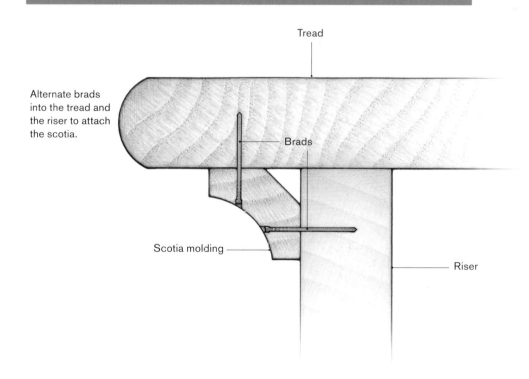

Tread

Alternate brads into the tread and the riser to attach the scotia.

Brads

Scotia molding

Riser

Simplified Measuring

Trying to get an exact length for a piece of molding under a tread overhang can be frustrating and difficult. Here are a couple of ways to make the process go more smoothly. First, measure over a specific distance, say 20 in., and mark that measurement on the riser. Then measure over from the other side to your mark and add the two measurements for your total length. The second way is similar, except instead of measuring in each direction, you start with a stick that is a given length and then measure over to the end of the stick.

Measuring in tight areas such as between skirts and under tread nosings can be awkward. One way is to first measure a set distance from one side (top right), then measure from the other side and add the two measurements together (right). Another way to make the same measurement is to use a stick that is a specific length, measure the leftover distance, and then add the two lengths together (bottom right).

wall. The handrail also has to have a profile that is "grip-able," and the ends of the handrail have to return to the wall so they don't snag anything. For this stair, the handrail was a preapproved shape, and it was just a matter of installing it in a code-approved manner.

Start by marking a plumb line up from the nosing of a tread near the bottom of the stair. Measure up 34 in. (the minimum code-approved height for the top of the rail), and then subtract the thickness of the railing and mark that point. Repeat the process at the top of the stair and at a tread in the middle of the stair, and snap a line through the points.

To position the brackets, first locate the wall studs or blocking to give the handrail firm support. Then set a block of wood on the line and slide a bracket up to it.

Hold the bracket in place over the stud location and mark the position of the holes. Drive a nail at each hole location to confirm that each screw is going into the stud. Then screw the brackets to the wall at the top, bottom, and middle of the stair (see the photos on p. 176).

Measure over from the wall to the middle one of the brackets. Now add half the width of the handrail stock to give you the length of the handrail return to the long point. With another crewmember holding

To set the height of the handrail, draw a plumb line up from the top and bottom tread nosings (below left). Then measure up and mark 34 in. for the minimum height of the handrail. Measure and mark the bottom of the handrail as well (below right).

the end of the tape, measure the overall length of the handrail that you'll need. The handrail should be roughly as long as the skirt board. Start by squaring one end of the handrail stock. Then mark the length of the return and make a 45-degree angle cut at that mark. Now flip the blade of your miter saw to 45 degrees in the opposite direction and make the end cut for the railing. The return should automatically space the railing at the proper distance from the wall. Glue and nail the return to the railing with light-gauge brads. The nails hold the return in place until the glue cures.

When the railing is ready to be installed, set it on top of the brackets and have a crewmember hold it in the proper position and against the wall while you screw the bracket to the railing, predrilling each hole beforehand. The stairway is now complete and up to code. By the way, these are the basics for the simplest stair with walls on both sides. Installing a stair rail with balusters is a chapter for another day.

 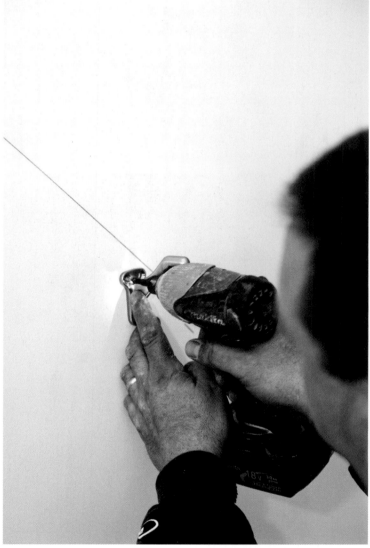

Snap a chalkline through the handrail marks you just made. Then position a scrap of wood with a square end on the line and line up the handrail bracket on a stud location (above left). Drive the screws for the bracket, making sure they all hit a stud or blocking (above right).

One crewmember holds the handrail against the wall in the right position while another crewmember secures the bracket to the railing.

Measure the distance from the wall to the handrail and make a right-angle return to hold the railing at that distance (top left). The return is required by code to keep objects from catching on the railing. Glue and nail the return to the railing (left).

Baseboard and Closets

So far we've discussed in detail most of the major carpentry and building projects to finish the inside of your home. There are a couple of smaller items to discuss, both of which are necessary to complete the inside of your home. We've mentioned baseboard and how it relates to the stair trim and other parts of the interior finish, but we need to do a step-by-step discussion of installing baseboard. We're also left with the closets, which can be a simple pole and shelf or can involve incredibly complex built-in cabinetry. We'll pick a treatment somewhere in the middle.

Installing Baseboard

Baseboard is thought of as one of the simplest tasks in finish carpentry, and there are countless stories of finish carpenters, first day on the job, being sent to a closet to run baseboard. Indeed, that is exactly where my professional carpentry career began—a bedroom closet in a little raised ranch in southern Rhode Island. According to legend, the new person is sent to work on an area where any mistakes will be less apparent. But I think the real idea is to put the new person in a tight and difficult place to work—where no one else *wants* to work! If you can survive the frustration of working in a closet, you're more likely to survive the rigors of finish carpentry over the long haul. But in a closet or not, with installing baseboard you get a chance to do (or to learn) a lot of the basic carpentry tasks: measuring, cutting, mitering, coping, and maybe even a little scribing.

Timing baseboard installation

We've discussed some tasks that should be done before baseboard is installed, especially flooring. Baseboard is the detail that completes the intersection of the walls and the floors. Installing baseboard over the flooring hides that joint in the easiest, most efficient manner. Baseboard also butts against the door casing, so the door openings should be cased before baseboard is run. However, the only thing stopping you from running baseboard on all those walls without doors is efficiency: It's much quicker to install all the baseboard in a room at the same time if at all possible. You might be prevented from completing all the baseboard at one time by things such as stair trim (as we saw in the last chapter), cabinets, and built-ins. Most finish carpenters that I know run the baseboard in each room as that room becomes completely ready.

Pros

Baseboard is one of the most basic of finish carpentry tasks. If you are an experienced finish carpenter, you can run baseboard in your sleep (and most of us have, instead of counting sheep!). If you are a novice and want to get your feet wet with the basics of finish carpentry, baseboard is the perfect opportunity.

Cons

I can think of only two reasons for not doing the baseboard yourself. The first reason is time. With all the other projects you need to do to finish your house, installing baseboard is an easy one to hand off with good expectations that the job will be done right with very little oversight. The second reason is sheer boredom. Running baseboard in room after room can get pretty monotonous. That said, baseboard is also one of those tasks that can go very quickly once you get into the installation groove.

Estimating the amount of baseboard material is fairly straightforward: Just count up the length of the walls in each room. As simple as that sounds, it's easy to overlook details such as the closets and those short returns from a corner to a door casing. When you have all the walls added up, add at least 10 percent for waste and for those areas that you might have failed to notice. And if your baseboard has more than one component, such as the baseboard described in this chapter, be sure to order enough of each component.

- Level
- Miter saw
- Compass scribes
- Coping saw
- Belt sander for cutting scribes

The baseboard in this room begins at the face of a decorative door casing instead of at the edge. Cut a slight miter angle on a scrap of baseboard so that it butts against the casing cleanly. Don't worry about matching the profile at this point; the base cap will complete that detail.

Start at a door

When a room is ready for baseboard, go around and mark the stud locations on all the walls. Then start at a doorway where the baseboard butts into the door casing. The baseboard in the photos shown here is a 1×6 topped with a decorative base cap molding. Usually the baseboard butts into the edge of the door casing, but for the room shown here, the door casing ran all the way into the corner. To meet the casing properly, the end of the baseboard had to be cut at a slight miter angle to fit tight against the profile. Cut that angle on a scrap of baseboard stock and place it in the corner against the casing. Measure from the opposite corner to the edge of the scrap. To cut that piece of baseboard, first cut the miter angle on a length of stock. Align the long point of the scrap with the long point on the angle you just cut, and measure the length from there. Because the base cap hides the corner, the lengths of baseboard can be slightly short, which also lets them slip into place easily.

Where the baseboard ends at a door casing, cut a piece slightly long to be cut to length later.

Continue cutting the pieces to the next door casing. Note that the last piece was not left long, and in this case, a new piece had to be cut to get the proper length.

At this point, the first length of baseboard is not ready to install. Instead, go around the room, cut all the pieces to length, and then set them in place against the wall. Determine the length for each piece by butting your tape against the preceding piece and measuring to the opposite corner. Where the baseboard ends at the next doorway, leave the piece a little long to be fit precisely later. In this room, the baseboard was interrupted by the closet door. After reaching one side of the closet door, we started at the other side and continued measuring and cutting the pieces over to the next door casing. Make sure the end that butts against the door casing fits at a precise angle. Discrepancies in the floor can alter the angle slightly. Begin with a square cut and scribe the end to take care of any gap that might be there.

The closet here was built into the room, which formed an outside corner. In a perfect world, all outside corners are exactly 90 degrees. To make the two sides meet perfectly, just make each side 45 degrees and the joint is perfect—just like the world, right? More typically, the corner bead and compound used by the drywall installers made the corner a little less than square. The best way to gauge the angle of the corner is to make pieces that are 1 in. or so longer than the length you need. Butt one end against the casing and then just trace along the corner bead. That gives you the short point of the angle. For the long point, set the intersecting length of baseboard on top of its mate and mark the point on each piece where the two lengths intersect. Connect the short and long points and you have your angle as well as your length.

For a precise fit against the floor, use a pencil flat against the floor and scribe the bottom edges of all the pieces in the room (above left). Clamp the baseboard to the miter-saw table and cut to the scribe line with a belt sander, adding a slight back bevel for a better fit (above).

Scribing to the floor

Recall that we sanded the edges of each room to make it easier for the baseboard installers. Although the sanding improved the situation, it didn't make for a perfectly even joint between the baseboard and floor. Having all the baseboard pieces cut and in place, look for the largest gap between the baseboard and the floor. That gap determines the amount that has to be taken off to make all the pieces sit perfectly flat against the floor. For this room, the largest gap was about 1/8 in., or about half the thickness of a pencil. So to make the joint as tight as possible, simply scribe the bottom of the baseboard by running a pencil flat along the floor (see the photos on the previous page).

There are many ways to cut to the scribe line. I used to use a small low-angle block plane. Some carpenters use a rasp. This crew clamped the length of baseboard to the miter-saw table and used a belt sander held perpendicular to the edge of the board. Use a moderate-grit sanding belt (80 grit to 120 grit)

on the sander, and work back and forth gradually until you reach the line. Get in the habit of leaving the line, and also angle the sander back slightly to create a back bevel. After scribing and cutting all of the pieces, set them in place and check the fit. If there are any places that still need to be taken down, mark them lightly, but just at the height of the line. At this point, you don't want to take the whole room down another 1/8 in.

When all the baseboard pieces are scribed to the floor satisfactorily, start with the first board and nail it in using two finish nails at each stud location. Work your way around the room until you get to the last piece that you left long earlier. With the preceding piece of baseboard nailed home, you can now get a precise length for the piece that finishes the run at the door casing. For this piece, first check the fit at the corner. If it isn't perfect, scribe and cut the end. Back in our perfect world, the baseboard always meets the casing perfectly square. But in reality, don't bet on it. Instead, align your steel rule with the bottom edge of

After scribing all the lengths of baseboard to the floor, attach each one using a pair of finish nails at each stud location.

To fit the final piece in each baseboard run, first scribe and cut the end that fits against the piece before.

the casing and draw a line out. Set the piece of baseboard in place extending past the edge of the casing. Mark the line for the bottom, and mark the top where it meets the casing as well. You can connect the two points and cut to the line, or if you have a miter saw equipped with a laser line, just set the angle so the laser line intersects the two marks. Apply a bead of carpenter's glue to both ends, slide the board into place, and nail it home.

On the other side of the closet door, recheck the fit of the outside corner pieces that were cut earlier. Then nail the first side in with four finish nails, remembering to glue the butt end against the door casing. With that side in place, apply glue to the face of the miter cut and nail the mating piece in place, starting from the corner and working toward the opposite end. If you made your cuts to fit perfectly, the corner should go together without nailing through the joint itself. When the corner is nailed home, wipe off the excess glue and sand the joint lightly.

To mark the other end of the final piece, first draw a line out from the edge of the casing (above). Set the piece against the casing and mark the top as well as the bottom line that you just drew (below left). Align the sawcut with the two marks and the piece should fit precisely (below).

Joining Two Boards for a Longer Length

When I did boat work, I first learned to join boards together to create a longer length. In the joinery shop, the technique was called scarfing, and with trim made from clear teak or mahogany, scarf joints would consist of long shallow angles to maximize the glue surface and to minimize the visual transition between the boards. The scarf joint for joining two sections of paint-grade baseboard together is easy by comparison. We just butt the pieces together with a glued biscuit for added strength.

To give the joint maximum support, make sure it is located over a stud. Measure and cut the first piece so it ends at a stud position. (By the way, it's better to have at least a couple of feet of stock on either side of the scarf joint, so locate the joint so you're not left with a short piece to add on.) Cut a slot for the biscuit and set the first piece in position. Scribe the first piece to the floor and nail it as you did the rest of the baseboard. Now measure and cut the piece of baseboard to complete that length. Use a dry-fit biscuit for alignment and slide the second piece into position. Get the scarf joint perfect, and then scribe the bottom of the second piece so it drops to the level of the first piece. Cut the scribe and double-check the fit.

Slather glue on both mating surfaces, especially in the biscuit groove. Be sure to spread glue all over the biscuit as well. Slide the piece into position and push the ends of the boards together until the joint is tight. Nail the second piece in, starting at the joint and working toward the opposite end. Wipe off the excess glue with a damp rag and sand the joint lightly.

To join two lengths of baseboard together, cut and install the first length with a slot for a biscuit cut in the end. The piece should end at a stud location (top). Cut the second piece and slide it into place using a dry biscuit to align it with the first piece. Scribe the bottom edge to put the two pieces at the same height (middle). Glue the ends and nail the second piece into place (above).

Base cap completes the profile

Many homes use just a simple square-edge or eased-edge board (with the edge rounded over slightly) as the finished baseboard. In this particular project, a decorative base cap molding was applied on top of the 1×6 base. The base cap is flexible and fits more tightly against the wall than the 1×6. A tighter fit means smaller gaps to fill and a neater-looking job. Plus, the base cap takes the decorative style of the baseboard up a notch to match the level of the window and door trim.

As with the 1×6, the first piece of base cap butted into the door casing profile, so it had to be scribed to the casing profile. Matching two different intersecting profiles meant first tracing the profile of the casing onto the end of the base cap and then cutting the shape with a coping saw. If you get a good fit the first time, then you're luckier than most. Most often you need to retrace and recut the end of the base cap until the two profiles meet with a very small gap that can be easily filled. Again, as you carve back to the scribe line with your coping saw, add a slight back bevel to make the joint look tighter.

To scribe the base cap to meet the door casing profile, first trace the shape as closely as possible on the end of the base cap (above right). Cut to the line with a coping saw (right). Repeat the process of tracing and cutting until the fit is satisfactory.

Because it's nearly impossible to get an overall length with the unusual scribe to the door casing, the best bet is to make up that length of base cap in two pieces. After getting the scribed end to fit satisfactorily, make a square cut on the other end and nail it in. Then it's just a matter of measuring from corner to corner for your length. This time it's important to cut the length exactly—there is no additional molding to hide any gap. In fact, because the other end of the base cap will be coped, make the length strong by a good $\frac{1}{16}$ in. (see the sidebar on p. 184).

Measure the next length from the opposite corner to the edge of the adjacent base cap (left). This measurement is to the short side of the 45-degree angle cut that begins the coped corner (below).

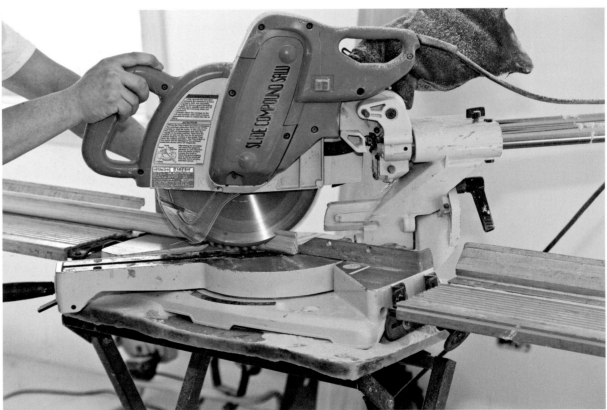

Coped corners

I mentioned earlier that baseboard was an opportunity to practice a lot of carpentry basics, including coped corners. I'm not sure who coped the first corner (probably an ancient Greek or Roman fitting moldings out of marble), but I want to meet that person and shake his hand (right after the person who invented the wheel). To understand the beauty of a coped corner, first consider what the joint would be if you didn't cope it. You would have to make two cuts at approximately 45 degrees (remember that drywall corners are seldom exactly square) and have the two sides meet perfectly. With a coped corner, the first side is cut square and extends all the way into the corner. Measure the second side to the edge base cap. That end of the base cap gets a 45-degree angle cut, so the measurement is to the short side of the 45-degree angle.

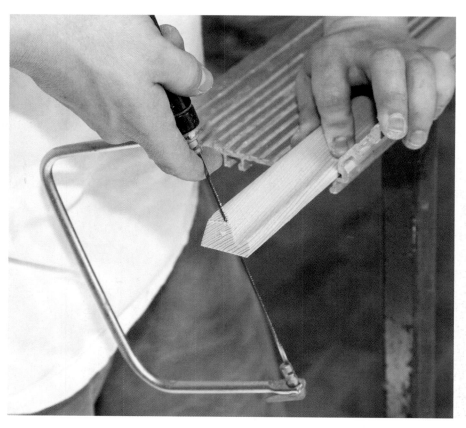

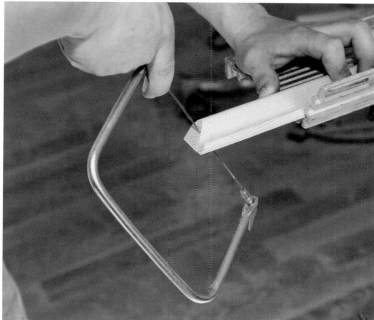

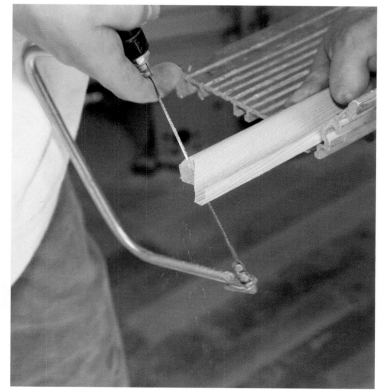

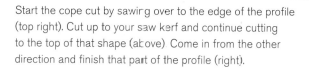

Start the cope cut by sawing over to the edge of the profile (top right). Cut up to your saw kerf and continue cutting to the top of that shape (above). Come in from the other direction and finish that part of the profile (right).

The coping part happens as you follow the line of the 45-degree profile with your coping saw perpendicular to the direction of the molding. Some profiles can be followed directly with the saw, but often it makes more sense to cut the meat of the profile first. Then plunge the blade in and follow the profile to your first cut. Continue your cut until the profile changes direction. Then come in from the other side to complete that part of the profile (see the photos on the previous page). Use the same approach for the other parts of the profile, cutting one direction first and then meeting the first cut from the other direction. Give the

TIP

Give the Molding a Little Spring

Sometimes a little extra pressure can help a coped corner close even more tightly. That extra pressure can come from cutting the piece slightly long. To put the piece into place, put one end in at a time, letting the middle spring out slightly. When the piece is nailed against the wall, that spring adds pressure to close the coped end completely.

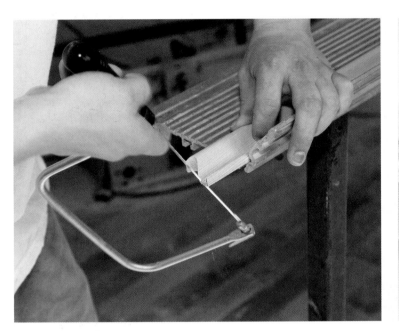

Complete the rest of the profile, working in from opposite directions (above left). Smooth the coping cut with a piece of sandpaper rolled into a tube shape (above). The coped piece should then fit tightly against its neighbor (left).

TIP

Folding Sandpaper

I've had a subscription to *Fine Woodworking* as long as I've been a subscriber to *Fine Homebuilding*. In one of the first issues of *FWW* that I bought, I learned a tip that I use to this day and show to people all the time. When you just fold a sheet of sandpaper on itself, the fresh grit on one face rubs on another, wearing it down before it can be used on wood. Instead, fold the sheet of sandpaper in half both ways, creating a cross of creases. Cut one of the creases from the middle out to the edge (it doesn't matter which crease). Now you can fold the paper into a more manageable quarter size without any sanding surface hitting another. When you wear out one surface, simply flip the paper over or refold the paper to expose another surface.

The best and most efficient way to use sandpaper is to fold the sheet in half in both directions. Then cut one of the four folds starting in the center (top). The paper can then be folded in on itself with no two abrasive surfaces touching (above).

Pros

Customizing a closet does not demand a lot of special skills or tools. Plus it can be a lot of fun and quite satisfying when you finish with special shelves to house your entire hat collection, or you finally have enough space for all your polo shirts and T's.

Cons

Again, if you don't have a lot of time, a pro can bang off a beautiful custom closet in a couple of hours. And you may be one of those people who is quite content with a simple shelf and pole.

TOOLS NEEDED

- Level
- Miter saw
- Tablesaw
- Driver drill

coping cuts a slight back bevel to ensure a tight fit, and when the cutting is done, smooth the cut with sandpaper rolled into a tube shape. The coped end should then nestle against the mating piece to form a neat joint (see the photos on p. 188).

To install the base cap, first run a bead of glue or construction adhesive along the back side, as well as on the coped end, and then spring the piece into place. Drive a 2½-in. finish nail at every stud location, angled down slightly to draw the base cap to the bottom board as well as against the wall.

Every room can be completed in this manner, including the closets if you plan to just put in a simple pole and shelf. But if you are considering a more complex closet system for better storage, then keep reading before you install the closet baseboard.

Closet Systems

The first closet that marked the humble beginning of my carpentry career was outfitted with just a closet pole and shelf. The pole was for hanging clothes and the shelf was for storing stuff that the homeowner probably wouldn't look at for years. That was the way we finished every closet, no matter what level house we were building. Installation was easy: Run a 1×4 or 1×6 cleat all the way around the closet 60 in. off the floor, add a shelf support in the middle (two if the closet was wide), closet pole brackets, a pole, and a shelf, and you were done. We should all have been arrested for wasting precious storage space!

Nail the base cap at a slight angle down at each stud location to draw the cap tightly against the bottom board.

ESTIMATING MATERIALS

Estimating the amount of material for a custom closet system means working off a plan (see the photo at right). Count up the linear feet for all the shelves and vertical supports and divide by 4 to get roughly the number of plywood sheets, then get an extra sheet of plywood just in case. Next, measure for the cleat stock. Like every other step, remember that this is an estimate—an exact number is not necessary.

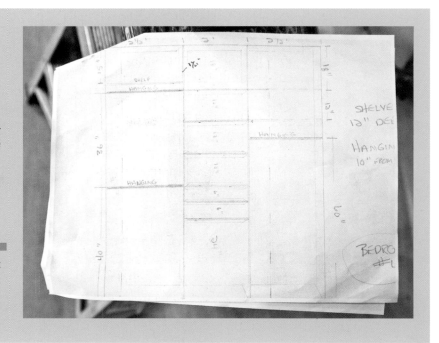

A quick sketch helps lay out and estimate materials for a custom closet system.

Start with a plan

The problem with the single shelf-and-pole system is that pants, shirts, and blouses don't generally need 60 in. of space to hang. In fact, 36 in. usually works just fine, which means that you can double the hanging space by putting in two poles: one above the other. But you always have some longer things to hang: dresses, dress pants, and so forth, so you'll need some full-height hanging as well. Most of us also need storage for nonhanging items—for me it's T-shirts and caps—so shelves that are more accessible make more sense than a single shelf that is too high to use effectively.

The good news is that it's pretty easy to customize a closet to your individual needs. The best thing is to start with a drawing or sketch. Don't drive yourself crazy trying to make a precise drawing, though. Count on making adjustments along the way as you build the system. For this closet, the middle shelf section was set at 24 in. wide, which meant efficient use of shelf stock. For the double-pole section on the left side, the top pole was set at 76 in. and the bottom pole at 40 in., giving the bottom section a little more clearance above the floor. The single pole on the right was set at the standard 60 in., and the shelves were set either 12 in. or 6 in. apart, with a 2-ft. space at the bottom for taller items, such a boots.

Look Out for Attic Access

In many homes, the access hatch for the attic space is located in a closet ceiling. If there is a hatch in one of your closets, think twice about an elaborate closet system that might interfere with using the hatch, especially if you have located machines such as air handlers in the attic. It would be unfortunate to have to tear out a beautiful closet system in an emergency to get a piece of equipment out of the attic.

The shelf section comes first

The vertical supports for the shelves determine the layout for the rest of the closet, so locate them first. To lay out their position, find the centerline of the closet wall, and then mark 12 in. on either side to center the 24-in. shelf section. Plumb down from those marks on one side with a vertical line to the floor (see the left photos on p. 192). The stock for the verticals as well as for the shelves was ¾-in. birch plywood. One of the challenges with this type of closet system is finding a way to attach the vertical supports: They are only ¾ in. wide where they meet the wall, and it would be pure luck if either vertical actually landed on solid framing. The answer is to attach the supports to the cleats (and

Lay out the position of the vertical shelf supports by finding the center of the closet and measuring 12 in. on either side (left). Plumb down from the line for the position of the first support (bottom left).

Mark the height of the top cleat on the plumb line (top), and then level over, marking the height in the corner and on the end wall of the closet (above).

to the baseboard) on either side of the shelves. Mark the height of the 1×6 cleat on the plumb line that you drew. A height of 63 in. puts the closet pole close to the requisite 60-in. height. Level over with a bubble level or with a laser and mark the height in the corner and along the end wall of the closet. Measure, cut, and install the back wall cleat, as well as the baseboard on that side of the shelf assembly. Rip the two supports

out of a 4×8 sheet of plywood, and along one edge of the support, mill the tongue for attaching the face trim with a slot-cutting bit in your router. Measure the height of the right support and cut it to fit. Scribe the support to fit the floor and ceiling if need be (see the tip below).

Set the first support in place against the cleat and the baseboard and mark the height of the top shelf.

Scribing to a Confined Space

To scribe a length that is closed at both ends, such as the shelf supports that fit between the closet floor and ceiling, cut the length long by ¼ inch or so. Then put the support in place at a slight floor-to-ceiling diagonal and make your scribe. Do the same procedure for both the floor and ceiling, scribing off half the extra length each time.

Cut and install the cleat as well as the baseboard on that side of the closet.

After fitting the first vertical support into place, measure up for the height of the top shelf, and then measure down from that point for the heights of the other shelves.

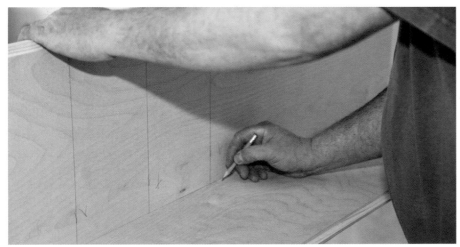

Place the end of the tape at that height and measure down for the heights of the rest of the shelves (see the right photo on p. 193). Don't install the first support just yet. Be sure that the floor is level between the positions of the two supports. If it is, then use the first support as a template for the second. Square the shelf heights across the first support and transfer the lines to the second. Be sure to put an "X" on the side of the line where the shelf is going. Set the first support back in position against the cleat and the baseboard, but still wait to install it.

Cut the shelf stock to length. In this case, the overall width was 24 in., so the length of the shelves was 24 in. minus the thickness of the two supports, or 22½ in. This strategy makes the shelves a little shorter, but it uses material more efficiently. If you make the shelves themselves 24 in. long, you would get only three complete shelves out of each 8-ft. length of plywood. Remember that every time you make a cut

Use the first shelf support as a template for the second (top) and transfer the shelf locations, being sure to mark an "X" on the side of the line that the shelf is going (left).

Using a Fence Stop for Repetitive Cuts

For the shelf section, a total of six shelves were needed. You could measure and mark each one, but that would be time-consuming, and there are bound to be tiny discrepancies in the lengths. A smarter solution is to use a stop, which attaches to the fence of the miter-saw stand. The stop allows you to make repeated cuts at precisely the same length. Factory-made stands such as the one in the photo at right always have a stop system, but you can also clamp or screw a block of wood to the side table as a stop.

Instead of measuring and cutting all the shelves separately, set the length using a stop to make every shelf exactly the same.

you lose about ⅛ in. to the saw kerf. It's frustrating (and wasteful) to discover that you only have 23⅝ in. left after cutting three 24-in. shelves.

Clear a nice open and flat area to work on, such as the outfeed table on a tablesaw. Place the back edge of the vertical support on the table and align one of the shelves with its layout line. Drive a finish nail near the front edge of the shelf, lining up the nailer with the center of the shelf by eye. The shelf now holds the vertical support in an upright position. As you might guess, lining the nailer up with the back edge of the shelf isn't as easy without some guidance. So square a line across the support that is centered on the shelf. Now the other fasteners can be driven safely into the middle of the shelf without guesswork.

Repeat this procedure at each of the shelves, tacking them in place with a finish nail and then squaring a line down for the second finish nail. When all the shelves are attached to the vertical support, go back and drive a couple of 2½-in. screws into each shelf using the same fastener lines. Because the shelves are in a closet and are being painted, the crew used regular coarse-thread drywall screws. A countersunk hole was drilled for each screw and the heads were

To preassemble the shelves to the second vertical support, first nail a shelf to the layout line. Then square a line down from the nail to guide the rest of the fasteners (above left). Fasten the bottom with a second nail to keep it on the layout line (above right), and drive a pair of screws to hold the shelf permanently in place (below).

driven just below the surface of the plywood. The holes were filled later, prior to painting.

When all the shelves are screwed to the support, carefully carry the assembly to the closet, positioning it against the other vertical support. Tack one of the shelves on its layout line and check to make sure that it's level. Now drive finish nails to attach the first support to the shelf cleat and to the baseboard. Tack the front edges of the rest of the shelves to their layout lines. Repeat the same procedure used earlier, squaring

lines across the support to align the fasteners. As before, drive an additional nail at the back of every shelf to hold the shelf on its line, and then drive screws to permanently attach the shelves to the support.

Cleats and side shelves

The shelf assembly is now built and attached to the cleat and baseboard on the right side that we installed earlier. Mark the height for the two pole cleats on the left side, extending the level lines to the corner as well

Check to make sure the shelves are level across (above), then nail the front edges of the shelves to the first support (below).

Complete the shelf system assembly by squaring lines across to guide the fasteners as before and then driving nails and screws into each shelf.

as across the end wall of the closet. After cutting both cleats for that side, apply construction adhesive to the back side of each, and then nail them in place with finish nails at each stud location. Now nail the shelf assembly to the cleats. Cut and install the baseboard for between the vertical supports, and nail the left support to the baseboard. Cut and install the rest of the cleat stock and baseboard in the closet, aligning the cleats to your level marks. Also add the cleats for the additional shelf on the right-hand side of the closet. Because these cleats don't need to support a closet pole, they can be made out of thinner stock.

Measure and install the shelves for side areas. If the closet seems to be a little out of square, this might be another good opportunity to use the stair-template tool. When the shelves are cut and fit, drive a screw through the shelf supports and into each shelf, making sure that the shelves are level.

Cut and install the closet-pole cleats for the other side of the shelf system (top left). Then nail the shelf support to the cleat (above). At the bottom, cut and install a piece of baseboard to go between the vertical supports, and then nail the second support to it (top right).

The cleat for the top shelf does not have to support a closet pole, so it can be made from narrower stock.

Cut the shelves and screw them to the vertical shelf supports.

Closet Trim Details

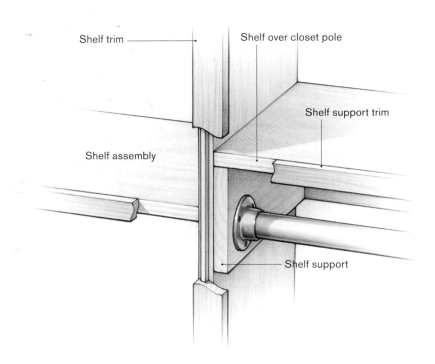

Shelf trim

Shelf over closet pole

Shelf support trim

Shelf assembly

Shelf support

Trim hides the plywood edges

At this point, all the major components of the closet system are installed except for the closet pole itself. The birch plywood is attractive and strong for the closet system, but the edges of the plywood can be vulnerable, and they are not easy to finish. The answer is to apply trim to all the plywood edges. Plywood is also subject to warping, and plywood shelves can sag if you put a lot of weight on them. A trim strip offers some support to keep those edges straight as well.

Recall that we milled a tongue on the edge of the vertical supports. That tongue is 3/8 in. deep and 1/4 in. wide. The trim for the vertical supports needs to have a matching groove that fits over the tongue. Mount the slot-cutting bit in your router, and mill the groove into the trim pieces for the two vertical supports. Cut both sides to length and dry-it them. Apply a healthy bead of glue to the groove and then install both trim pieces, using brads to hold them in place until the glue cures.

The trim pieces for the vertical supports are 1½ in. wide, with the extra ¾ in. of stock extending over the closet pole cleats. The extra width gives the trim added strength to resist warping. For all the shelves, the trim is 1 in. wide and 5/8 in. deep. The 1-in. width not only adds strength, but it also overlaps the bottom edge of the plywood for a cleaner look. The 5/8-in. dimension puts the finished edge of each shelf 1/8 in. behind the vertical supports. That lip creates a shadow line and offers a cleaner look than if you tried to make the surfaces flush. To make the shelf trim, first rip 1-in.-wide strips out of 1× stock, then rip each of them down to 5/8 in. By the way, it's much easier to rip shorter lengths, so figure out a rough length and cut as many strips as you'll need. And remember to always use a push stick when milling narrow strips on a tablesaw.

The quickest and most accurate way to get the lengths for the trim pieces is to set them in place and mark the length you need. Label each one so you know

To finish the edges of the plywood supports, rout a groove into the edge of the trim piece that fits over the tongue on each support.

Apply a bead of glue to the groove and nail the trim piece into place with a brad nailer.

where it goes, and then bring the whole pile to the miter saw, cutting them in one trip. Apply a bead of glue to the back side of each trim piece, and again use brads to hold the pieces in place until the glue cures.

Closet poles complete the job

The last step in the process is to mount the closet poles. The hangers for closet poles have stayed the same for as long as I've been doing carpentry. In the past, we used plastic versions of the hangers that did the job just fine, but this closet called for chrome-plated metal hangers. The bracket for one end of the pole is a closed circle, whereas the other end is U-shaped so the pole can drop down into the bracket.

We installed the cleats so the tops of the poles would be at the specified heights on the plan. Start

To make the trim for the shelves, first rip strips 1 in. wide, and then rip those strips to ⅝ in. thick.

Measure the length of each piece of shelf trim in place.

with one of the closed brackets and position it with the center of the bracket 10 in. from the back wall of the closet. Mark the outer edge of the mounting flange and measure to that mark. Each of the brackets is installed to that measurement to keep the poles parallel to the back of the closet. Holding the bracket at that measurement and at the right distance from the bottom of the cleat (¼ in.), punch starter holes for the three screws.

When all the brackets are installed, measure the length of the poles. When I outfitted closets, we always used wooden poles, but wooden poles need extra support to keep them from sagging. This closet used heavy-duty chrome-plated metal tube for the poles, which is a much heavier and stronger material than

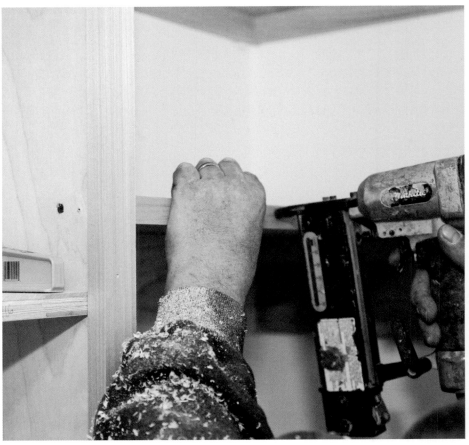

Then glue and nail the pieces to the shelves.

To position the closet pole brackets, set the first one at the proper distance from the back and mark the outer edge of the flange.

TIP

An Awl Holds the Bracket in Place

The tool to use for making the starter holes is an awl. When installing the circle brackets, position one of the holes at the top. Punch the bottom holes first, and the top hole last. Leave the awl stuck in the cleat to hold the pole bracket in position while you drive the bottom screws.

Set the rest of the brackets the same distance from the back of the closet. Use an awl to start holes for the screws. Let the awl hold the bracket through the top screw hole while the two bottom screws are driven.

wood, but also a lot more expensive. The poles have to be long enough so they don't slip out of the brackets, but short enough to drop into position without being forced. And with the pole stock as expensive as it is, we couldn't afford to make a mistake. So we cut test lengths from scraps of wooden strip. The strip could then be set directly on the pole to mark the right length.

With the V-groove facing up, set the pole stock in the holder (see the sidebar on the facing page). Clamp the pole through the protective plastic to keep from marring the surface. The clamp holds the closet pole stationary, so you can cut it to length with a reciprocating saw. Use a file to remove any burr left from the cutting, and the pole should then drop easily into place.

Use a scrap strip of wood to determine the exact length of the closet pole.

Remove any burrs or rough edges from cutting the closet pole, and it should slip easily into the brackets.

TIP

Holding the Pole for Cutting

Cutting metal pole can be tricky. A hacksaw would work well but would take a long time. The best option is a metal-cutting blade in a reciprocating saw. But the tricky part comes in holding the round metal tube stationary while you make the cut, without marring the shiny finish on the pole. To make the holder, make opposing 45-degree-angle cuts along the center of a scrap piece of 2×4 about 18 in. long. To make the cuts, set the blade on a tablesaw to 45 degrees, cutting about ¾ in. deep. Cut one side, then flip the board to cut the other side.

To hold the closet pole stationary for cutting without marring the surface, make a holding board with a V-cut down the middle (above). Set the pole in the V, clamp it in place through the protective plastic, and cut the pole with a metal-cutting blade in a reciprocating saw (below).

10

Painting

When I worked as a contractor, I left most of my painting to the pros. Painting always frustrated me, as I seemed to get more paint on me than I did on what I was supposed to be painting. The pros did a cleaner, faster, and, quite frankly, more professional-looking job. But as with every other aspect of building, I picked the brains of my subs and got more comfortable and confident with my painting. Although I consider myself a carpenter above all else, I've often thought that being a professional painter would be the trade I'd enjoy most at this stage in my life. The job is quiet for the most part, and except for spending time on ladders and scaffolding, painting is pretty safe. It's also satisfying to be the trade that completes the work of home building.

Pros

There are two types of people in this world: those that enjoy painting and those that hate it. I count myself in the former group. If you're on the fence about painting, perhaps some professional advice and guidance could make you an enjoyer.

Cons

Like every other step in finishing a house, painting will go more quickly if done by a professional, so if you're pressed for time, don't try to rush this crucial step. And if you are one of the aforementioned painting haters, leave this job to the pros.

- Good brushes (see the sidebar on p. 210)
- Good paint rollers and roller frames
- Extension handle for the paint roller
- 5-in-1 tool
- Sandpaper
- Clean rags

Estimating paint coverage isn't that hard. Count up the square footage of the walls in each room and for each color. Tell your paint supplier how much you need to cover and round up to the nearest gallon. Count up the square footage of ceilings separately and have your supplier figure out the amount of ceiling paint as well. Be aware of the finishes you'll need: I always use semi-gloss for trim and eggshell for the walls and ceilings. If you didn't have your drywall installer prime the walls and ceilings, you'll need to order primer as well.

Prep Work Is the Most Important Step

A wonderfully wise craftsman named Charlie Tuttle once told me that preparation is 9/10 of every job. There is no part of home building where this is truer than with painting. Before you pop the top on that can of paint, there is a lot of preparation that has to be done so the job goes quickly, smoothly, and neatly.

Site preparation

The first thing to consider before you paint a room is what you *don't* want to paint. The biggest item on that list is the floors. When the drywall installers primed the walls and ceilings, preparation was just a matter of covering the windows—the finished flooring had not been installed at that point. But with the flooring now installed, it has to be covered before you paint the walls and trim. You can use canvas drop cloths, but they don't sit tight to the edge of the floor for painting the baseboard. You should avoid plastic drop cloths because they can be very slippery underfoot. A better alternative is to cover the entire floor with red rosin paper, taping the edges right up to the baseboard (see the top left photo on p. 206). Red rosin paper is inexpensive, resists spills, and it isn't slippery underfoot. If installed carefully, a layer of red rosin paper can protect the floors through the entire messy process of painting.

The next thing to do is to remove the hardware from the windows. If the hardware is interchangeable between the windows, put it all in a plastic bag or a box along with all the screws and put the box away for

The best way to keep the finished floors safe during painting is to cover the entire floor with red rosin paper. That way the floors are protected from splash, splatter, and spillage that can occur during every phase of painting.

safe keeping. Any hardware for a specific window or door should be put in its own box or bag and labeled. The more methodical and thorough you are with this process, the easier it will be to find and reinstall the hardware when the painting is finished.

The crew that painted the project in the photos shown here also removed the doors to be painted separately. Recall that you spent a lot of good time and effort hanging each door and getting it to fit and swing properly. So each door should stay matched to its specific opening. As you take each door off, remove the hinges and store them with their screws in a specific box or bag, just as you did with the window hardware. Number each door and write the number in the hinge locations on both the jamb and the door itself. Take the doors to a single location to be painted, stacking them in the same direction for easy reference.

Painting door trim and doors is much easier with the doors removed. First remove each door from its opening and number the opening (top right). Remove the hinges from the door and number the door as well. Stack the doors in one place where they will be painted at the same time (right).

Filling holes

As a carpenter, one of the jobs I hated the most was filling nail holes. It was the most tedious of the finishing jobs, and inevitably when I opened the container of spackle or filler it was hard and dry and difficult to work with. And those places where I'd driven three nails and made three holes now took three times as long to fill. The process did, however, make me much more careful about overzealous nailing.

When filling holes, use a good-quality putty or spackling that won't shrink. No need to repeat the tedium twice. I always used (or tried to use) a putty knife to apply the filler. But the knife pulled the filler out of the hole as it passed over, so it always took too many passes to fill. In the end, I'd put a dab of putty on my fingers, pushing it into the hole and rubbing it smooth. The painting crew for this project was smart. They bypassed the whole putty-knife step and just applied the spackling with their fingers.

After dispensing a small amount of fresh spackle into a small container such as a paper cup, press a dab of spackling into the nail hole, then rub back and forth lightly to remove the excess. The key word here is lightly. Rub too hard and you'll pull the spackle out of the hole. Don't go crazy trying to get the spackle perfectly smooth because you'll go back over it with sandpaper later. Work methodically around the room, working your way along the baseboard as well as around every door and window. This step is where consistency in your carpentry pays off. For example, if you used two nails at every stud, at approximately the same distance from the top and bottom of each length of baseboard, you can fill the holes very quickly and be assured that you haven't missed any. If your nails were all over the place, filling the holes takes longer as you hunt for every stray hole.

Sanding spackle

The next step is to sand off the excess spackle. The spackle should be ready to sand after about an hour. Use fine sandpaper, such as 120 grit, and fold it the same as we did for the finish carpentry (see "Folding

It may look messy, but the best way to apply spackle is with your finger. Press a dab of spackle into the nail hole, then rub lightly to remove the excess.

Sandpaper" on p. 189). Use the sandpaper on the flat for the flat sections of the molding profiles. The casing has deep beads that inevitably catch excess spackle. Use the folded edge of the sandpaper to smooth those areas (see the top photo on p. 208). For rounded edges such as the windowsill, let the sandpaper wrap evenly around the profile as you sand. Just as with filling the holes, work in a methodical pattern to make sure all the holes get sanded smooth with the excess spackle removed.

Sand the spackle as well as all the trim surfaces at once. Use the sandpaper on the flat for the wide, even parts of the trim. For narrow parts of the profile such as a bead, use a fold in the edge of the sandpaper. Let the sandpaper wrap around areas such as the windowsill and rounded edges of the apron.

Caulk the edges

When I first started in the trades, caulk had one purpose: weather sealing. Imagine my surprise the first time I saw a painter whip out his caulking gun and fill the gap between the trim and the wallboard. An aesthetic use for caulking—what a great concept! The caulk creates a perfectly smooth transition between the two surfaces.

The trick to applying caulk is to dispense a small, controlled amount. Cut the nozzle of the tube with a utility knife to create a diagonal opening about ⅛ in. wide. A good-quality caulking gun is also a big help. Better guns are easier to load and won't wear out your hand squeezing the handle. Caulk has a limited working time, so work one seam at a time. For a window, start at the top of the casing and work your way down. Keep the nozzle in contact with both surfaces at about a 45-degree angle from the wall. Move slowly and steadily, dispensing an even bead without excess caulk building up around the nozzle. Wet your finger and run your finger down the bead, creating a tooled corner in the radius of your fingertip.

Apply a bead of caulk along the joint between the trim and the wallboard (top). Then wet your finger, and use the curve of your finger to tool the caulk into the joint (above).

Choosing Caulk

There is a staggering number of caulks on the market with some very specific purposes. To fill gaps between the trim and drywall, choose an adhesive caulk with the following attributes: fast drying, adheres to most surfaces, easy cleanup, and, above all, paintable. Caulk also comes in colors, so choose a color that your paint will cover easily.

Caulk every joint where the trim meets the drywall, including along the window and door casings (don't forget the top edge of the casing), the bottom of the apron, and along the top edge of the base cap molding. Other places that should be caulked are the baseboard corners, including the coped base cap corners. Also caulk the seams where two moldings meet, such as the baseboard and door casing. Caulk fills and smoothes difficult transitions, such as where the base cap was scribed into the profile of the casing.

Dust, sweep, and vacuum

The final step before you start to paint is a total cleanup of all surfaces to remove dust and debris from the sanding and filling process. Start with the walls and wipe them down with a rag. A slightly damp rag works best. Dust and vacuum the trim around each window and door, getting into all the beads and the corners where construction dust can accumulate. Pay close attention to horizontal surfaces such as windowsills. Also take time to dust all the muntins (the wooden strips that separate the panes) on each window. If there is any stuck-on debris such as dried drywall compound, remove it now, sand lightly, and then clean up the dust and debris. Most craftspeople that I know run their hands along the surfaces feeling for any irregularities or debris. Now is the time to remedy any problem areas. It's never fun if you have to interrupt the painting process to sand off a chunk of debris.

Caulk the intersection of trim boards, such as in a corner, or where the baseboard butts into a door casing.

Painting Windows and Doors

Just mention those words, and some people can feel their pulse jumping up a notch. I know the feeling because I used to be there. But then I began to learn the Zen of painting, especially painting with a brush. It may sound like hooey, but once you learn the "feel" of the brush, painting can turn from drudgery to joy. That's right, you will actually enjoy painting. Most of the art of painting is how to use the brush: how to hold it, how to load it, when to use the widest part of the bristles, when to use the narrow profile, and so on.

Types of brushes

If you're like me, the first time I looked at the selection of brushes available for sale, I almost broke into a cold sweat: different types of bristles, different widths, different handles, some with the bristles at an angle, and huge difference in prices—Yikes! I took a deep breath and started with the type of paint I would be using. Like most of us, I needed a paintbrush that I could use for both oil and latex paints, so I chose brushes with synthetic bristles clearly labeled, "For all paints."

Next, I chose the width I'd need. The timid person usually chooses a narrow brush thinking that a narrow brush gives you more control. I bought a 1½-in. brush and a 2½-in. brush, but rarely use the smaller one. That's because once I learned how to control the brush, the width of the brush did not matter. I've noticed that most professional painters use a 3-in. brush for all their work, except when they're in extremely tight quarters. When it comes to handles, I like the feel of unfinished wood. An unfinished wooden handle is also pretty easy to keep clean and free of paint.

Brushes with bristles cut at an angle are known as sash brushes, probably because the pointed end of the bristles is supposed to make painting all the parts of a window easier. But that theory isn't always true. In fact, standard square brushes give you the advantage of being able to use both ends of the brush with one loading. That said, I stubbornly stick to my 2½-in. sash brush because I like the way it feels, and it has always done a wonderful job for me.

The nonbelievers out there are still shaking their heads. Why go to all that expense and fuss when you can pick up a "chip" brush for two bucks and just toss it when you're done? My answer is partly a matter of pride in tool ownership. If I'd bought a disposable brush every time I needed to paint—instead of my good brush—I'd have thrown away a small mountain of brushes, which is both wasteful and expensive. The other reason is that a good paintbrush just does a better job, period. The paint goes on more smoothly

Start with a Good Brush

A while back, one of my painting contractors took me aside and gave me two cardinal rules of painting: First, always use top-quality paint, and second, buy the best brushes and treat them with the same respect and maintenance as you do the rest of your tools. Trusting his word, I went out and got a couple of good brushes that set me back almost $20 apiece. I also bought a good wire brush and a comb for cleaning the brushes. I still have those brushes, and they work as well today as they did over 20 years ago due to my diligence in keeping them clean and ready for use.

Not sure what the best brush is? Ask your paint supplier for his guidance, or ask a painting contractor what brushes he or she uses and why.

Almost 25 years old and still going strong. Bought in the late 1980s, these two paintbrushes have been used for dozens of paint jobs. Diligent maintenance has kept them in great shape.

TIP

Don't Throw Out the Packaging

If you've just gone out and bought your first good paintbrush, you probably pulled off the cute little bristle cover and tossed it. Go back and dig it out of the trash. Keep that cover to protect your brush for as long as you own it. (More on that topic when we get to cleaning a paintbrush.)

with less streaks, and a good paintbrush does not shed bristles. There is nothing more frustrating than going back to your paint job and finding a bristle dried in the surface. I cannot tell you the last time one of my brushes lost a bristle—it simply does not happen.

Holding a paintbrush

So you bought a good brush and now you just pop the top on the paint can, dip, and go, right? Not so fast. Before you start painting, take your brush out (dry) and hold it in your hand to learn a few basic grips. For the standard grip that you'll use most of the time, hold the brush as if it is a large pencil with the handle resting between your thumb and first finger. Your other fingers should rest on the ferrule or the wood above the ferrule. Your grip should be light and the brush should feel like an extension of your hand. This grip should allow you to brush in both directions comfortably, and rotating your wrist allows you to brush with the bristles edgewise.

As with any technique, you'll need to adjust your grip until it's most comfortable, and as you paint, you'll find that you change your grip to fit certain situations. When you need to reach above you, try sliding your hand farther down the handle, keeping your forefinger on the handle for more control. This grip is also helpful in areas where your hand might block the view of the bristles, which is critical for accurate painting. Yet another variation is sort of a backhand version of the same grip with the handle resting lightly in the palm of your hand. Again, the

The most common grip for a paintbrush is with the handle between your thumb and forefinger and your fingers resting on the ferrule. With this grip, turning your wrist 90 degrees allows you to paint with the edge of the brush.

For extended reach, slide your fingers down the handle. This grip is helpful when the normal grip might block your view of the bristles, such as in painting this muntin.

most important thing here is to maintain a feather-light touch with minimal pressure. Remember that the brush is a paint delivery tool. Just touching the surface lightly should cause the paint to flow out of the brush.

A third variation is sort of a backhand version of the handle grip. The most important factor when holding a paintbrush is maintaining a light touch.

Loading the brush

It's time to smell the paint for the first time. Open the paint can using your 5-in-1 tool. Just like every other task, there is a knack to opening a can of paint. Insert the tool into the groove between the lid and the can

and pry up lightly to break the seal. Now move around the can a couple of inches and pry up a little more. Keep working around the can until the lid is loose. Be gentle! Being too aggressive can distort the lid, and if you need to reuse it, it won't seal back on the can properly.

Give the paint a stir. Even if the can has been shaken by the paint supplier's machine, it's a good habit to get into to ensure a complete and even mix. As you remove the stirring stick, keep brushing the paint off the stick and back into the can. Now just dip the brush in, scrape it on the edge, and paint, right? WRONG! This is perhaps the single biggest mistake made by nonprofessional painters. I cannot think of a single situation where I would recommend working directly out of a paint can. Instead, work out of a clean paint bucket. Paint supply houses sell plastic paint buckets very inexpensively, or you can make your own (see the sidebar below). One of the big advantages to working out of a bucket this way is weight. It's much easier on your arms and hands if you don't have to hold a heavy can, and there is much less chance for a spillage accident as well.

Pour an inch or two of paint into the bucket. I always pour toward the brand-name side, leaving the instructions side high and dry. (I'm always afraid I'll need to read the manufacturer's notes at some point, and I don't want them covered in paint.) Have your

Making a Paint Bucket

While at *Fine Homebuilding*, I had the good fortune to work with Brian Doherty, a professional painter in Virginia. Brian was the first to drive home the concept of working out of a separate bucket while you paint. Brian always made his buckets out of used paint cans. He used his 5-in-1 tool as a can opener and cut the rim off the can. He then flattened any burrs from the opening process, and he had a bucket ready for service.

Never work directly out of the paint can. Instead, buy a bucket, or you can cut the rim out of a used paint can and make your own.

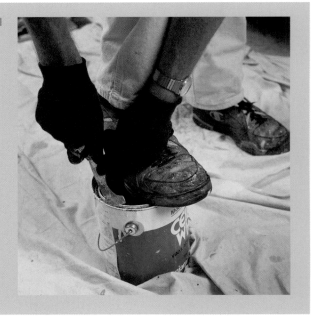

brush ready to wipe the excess paint off the side of the can and out of the lip as well. Set the lid back on the paint can to keep air and airborne debris away from the paint. Dip the brush into the paint about 1 in. deep. Most folks go right for the scrape on the edge, but don't you dare. If you dip and scrape, you're just coating the outside of the brush and then scraping it off. Very little paint actually gets into the brush, and if you scrape only one side, that side will have no paint while paint is dripping off the other side—a sure recipe for a mess.

Instead, lightly tap the side of the can, one side then the other. Tapping forces the paint *into* the bristles, loading the brush with paint. Now when you touch the surface, paint flows *out of* instead of *off of* the brush. You also have some time before paint starts to drip out of the brush, and if you're working with the brush above you, the paint won't run back down over the ferrule and handle. Every time you need more paint, dip and tap, dip and tap. I guarantee that your painting projects (and your hands) will be much neater once you master this technique. And now I'm finally going to let you do some painting.

Prime first if necessary

I'm going to discuss painting with a paintbrush in the context of painting a window. All the techniques used here apply to every other aspect of painting trim. Most new windows these days come with the sashes and

To load your brush properly with paint, first dip it into the bucket about an inch or so (far left). Tap the bristles against one side, and then the other (above and left). The tapping forces the paint from the outside of the bristles to the inside where it can flow out evenly without dripping.

jambs primed, but the casing, sill, and apron that you installed are raw wood and will need to be primed.

The most difficult part of brushing paint on is a process known as cutting in—painting to an edge in a straight line without getting paint on the adjacent surface. Not only do you have to cut in the wall next to a trim board, but you'll also have to cut in along that board next to a wall. All the window muntins have to be cut in along the edges of every pane, and if there are plastic or metal runners along the jambs, you'll need to cut in to those as well. With the walls primed, but without a finish coat, the primer on the windows can be cut in quickly, without making an absolutely perfect line. The finish coats on the trim and subsequent finish coats on the wall are the times to cut in more carefully. That said, still try to cut in the primer in a fairly neat line. The other parts of the casing can be painted in the regular fashion, overlapping the primer onto the primed jambs without worry.

Overlap the primer onto the factory-primed jambs.

With multiple coats to follow on both the walls and trim, cutting in with the primer does not have to follow a dead accurate line.

Finish coats of paint require more care

When the primer is dry, go back and lightly sand all the surfaces, including the factory-primed areas. Most new windows these days can be tilted in for cleaning. This feature also helps the painter access parts of the window that might be more difficult to get at for sanding and for painting. When you are finished sanding, go back and dust off the entire window (a task worthy of a cheap paintbrush). Now you're ready for the finish paint.

You need to follow a certain order to paint the entire window without having two painted surfaces touch and without getting your fingers in the wet paint. Start with the window trim. Begin brushing from the 45-degree mitered corner along the face of the casing. That way, the brush strokes stay parallel to the direction of the trim piece. Paint the adjacent piece from the corner, starting at the same line. To get paint into the deep parts of the casing profile, turn your brush on edge and apply a little more pressure to make the bristles penetrate farther. When you've coated an area, go over it lightly, brushing in the same direction to smooth out the brushstroke lines. To complete one section of trim, brush lightly from one end and then from the other end, lifting the brush as you overlap the strokes from the other direction.

For this coat, cut in the lines carefully. To cut in a line such as the edge of the casing, load your brush with just a little paint. Put the brush on the edge of the casing and press until the tip of the brush squeezes over to the line. Then draw the brush along. Note that at this point, just the bristles at the end are doing the painting. When the brush starts running out of paint, draw the bristles back from the edge and smooth out the strokes you just made. The tendency is to go too slowly with the brush along the edge. But the more slowly you go, the better chance there is for the natural shakiness in your hand to make a line that isn't straight. For tricky little corners such as where the apron returns to the wall, tap the brush without dipping it first. That redistributes the paint already in the brush. Then just let the end few bristles press into

Paint each piece of trim parallel to its grain. Start at the miter joint and work down for a jamb casing (top). To get paint all the way into a profile such as the edge bead on this casing, turn your brush on edge and apply a little pressure (middle).

Finish painting each area with a feather-light stroke to create an even layer of paint and to smooth out the brush marks.

For accurate cutting in, place the tip of the paintbrush on the edge of the trim. Press lightly until the edge of the brush reaches the line you are cutting to. Then draw the brush steadily and evenly along the line.

the corner. A good brush will separate in this manner and turn into a fine artist's brush in an instant.

Painting muntins

When I renovated my bathroom in Connecticut, I got the brilliant idea that if I put French-style doors on the linen closet, the visibility would force us to keep the closet in order. Luckily I'd just finished an article on painting with Mr. Doherty, and was feeling very confident in my painting abilities. Good thing, each of the doors had 10 panes that I had to paint around with three coats of paint on both sides. By the time I was finished I could paint around a window with the best of them.

For those of you expecting a lesson on how to tape off a window, you're going to be disappointed. Taping takes a long time to do properly, and even the best taping job allows paint to seep under here and there, which requires cleanup time. Instead, just "feel the Force" and cut in all the muntins with your paintbrush.

We mentioned before the importance of completing a window in the right order. So far we've painted the casings and jambs over to the window tracks. We've also painted the sill and apron. Start the actual window by pulling the top sash down slightly and painting the muntins around the top panes. Again, use just a small amount of paint in your brush, and gently splay the bristles into the corner. The bristles separate, and as before, you end up painting with a brush that is just a small portion of the whole brush. With each side of each muntin, start in the corner and paint toward the middle. The side muntins are longer and wider, so it's possible to use the whole brush on them.

When you've painted around the top panes, paint the front of the sash as well. Push the top sash down and the bottom sash up so you can paint around the bottom panes of the top sash. Finish painting all surfaces on that sash, and don't forget the primed part of the sash that is covered when the window is closed. Now you can paint around all the panes of the bottom sash, but don't paint the very top of the sash yet. Don't forget to paint the primed areas on the bottom of the sash as well.

When the bottom sash is all painted except for the top edge, pull the sash forward in its cleaning position. Now you can paint the last of the window guide strips. When they are painted, push the sash back into position and paint the top edge. The entire window has its first finish coat and there are no fingerprints in the fresh paint.

Second coat, same as the first

When the first coat is dry, give it a light sanding with 220-grit sandpaper. The sanding smoothes out any imperfections in the surface and also takes the luster off the first coat to prepare for the second. The second coat goes on in exactly the same order as the first. The second coat generally goes on more quickly. If you've done a good job cutting in the edges and filling in the profile, you can just run the brush close to the edge of your first cutting-in line. The important thing on the second coat is to cover every surface completely and feather your brush to leave a mirror-smooth finish.

The Zen of Painting Window Sash

1

Begin painting a window sash by painting around the top panes of the top sash. Press the tip of the bristles lightly into the corner next to the glass. The bristles will separate naturally, creating a smaller brush to control for this fine work.

2

The vertical muntins can be painted with the whole edge of the bristles.

3

When you've finished the top of the top sash, reverse the sashes and paint around the bottom panes.

Don't forget to paint places that will be covered once the window is closed.

4

Now paint around all the panes of the bottom sash (left). Paint the bottom of the sash as well, but don't paint the top of the sash yet (below).

5 6

Tip the bottom sash into the cleaning position and paint the guide strips on either side. When you're finished, tip the sash back up and paint the top of the sash.

Cleanup is the final step

One of my biggest pet peeves is walking onto a job site or into a workshop and seeing handles of paintbrushes sticking out of a coffee can full of rusty water. "Oh, I'll clean that brush tomorrow..." But as they say, tomorrow never comes and those brushes are doomed. Plan ahead and *always* take the time to clean your paintbrushes thoroughly and methodically after every use—I often clean mine between coats. By the way, the cleanup method described here is for water-based latex paint only.

When you're finished painting, dump the excess paint back in the paint can. I always use my brush as a

TIP

Drips Happen

Even the best painters sometimes apply too much paint or apply paint unevenly. That is when drips occur. The best way to prevent drips is to apply a thin, even layer of paint and then to feather the final strokes. If a drip or sag occurs unnoticed and dries, it is very difficult to hide. So always keep an eye out for them. When you see a drip forming, you can go after it with a rag, but that usually messes up a large area around the drip as well. The best way to fix a drip is with your paintbrush. First empty the brush as much as possible. I've even painted the side of a cardboard box or a piece of plywood to get as much paint out of the brush as I could. Then you can go over the drip, and the paintbrush will soak up the excess paint. If there is a lot of extra paint, you may have to go over the spot a couple of times. Just as before, feather the final strokes and breathe a sigh of relief that you caught the drip before it was too late.

Sand in between finish coats of paint with 220-grit sandpaper to smooth out any irregularities and to take the luster off the first coat.

Brush on the second coat in exactly the same order as the first.

mop to get as much paint as possible and squeeze it back into the can. For the record, this is the only time I let myself scrape the brush on the lip of the can. If you've been painting for a few hours, there may be dried or skinned paint on the sides of the bucket. Make sure none of that stuff gets into the paint can. It does not dissolve and if it ends up on your brush or roller, it can mess up your next paint job.

Fill the bucket about halfway with water. I use the brush as a scrubber and clean the sides of the bucket as thoroughly as possible. Dump the bucket, pour in fresh water, and give the bucket another scrub. At this point the water should be less cloudy. Now use a wire brush to scrub the bristles. I know this must sound like paintbrush torture, but trust me, it is the best way to clean a paintbrush, and it doesn't seem to harm the brush at all. Rinse the brush in the water and go at it again with the wire brush. Be sure to scrub extra hard up by the ferrule, and continue scrubbing and rinsing with fresh water until all the flecks of paint are gone from the bristles.

Pour fresh water into the bucket and rinse the bristles thoroughly. Squeeze out the water and check the color. If the water coming out of the bristles is cloudy, keep rinsing. If the brush is particularly dirty, scrub it with the wire brush again. Rinse and squeeze until the water from the bristles is clear. Then put the

handle between your hands and rub it back and forth rapidly to spin the brush and dry the bristles. I use a retired kitchen sponge with an abrasive pad on one side to clean the handle and ferrule thoroughly. As a final step, go through the brush with a brush comb, and then let it dry thoroughly. When it's dry, slip the manufacturer's cover back over the brush. The cover keeps dirt and debris out of the bristles, and it maintains the shape of the brush so it's ready for the next job.

Rinse the brush and squeeze the water out of the bristles. The first rinses will yield cloudy water. Continue rinsing and scrubbing until the water comes out of the brush clear.

Use a wire brush to remove any paint adhering to the bristles.

Place the handle of the brush between your hands and spin the brush by rubbing your hands together. This action removes most of the water from the bristles.

When the brush is mostly dry, comb the bristles to straighten them.

Painting Walls

There was a reason behind starting my discussion of painting with windows. Once you've mastered painting windows with a paintbrush, cutting in for painting walls is a piece of cake. Just as with painting windows, be sure you prepare properly. The walls for this project were primed by the drywall installers, but the primed surface needed to be sanded. You can sand walls by hand, but a machine attached to a vacuum does a faster, cleaner, and more efficient job. Sanding machines are usually available for rent.

Cutting in

Cutting in around walls always makes me worry. There is so much to do: along the ceiling, along the baseboard, around doors, around windows, corners, and electrical boxes. I try to work my way around a room methodically, but with so much cutting in to do, the first paint I apply is dry by the time I get all the way around the room, and it has changed color by a few shades. I'm always relieved when the fresh paint from the roller dries seamlessly with the cut-in areas.

I usually start cutting in the wall–ceiling joint. With walls, you want to cover enough area so the

Trim First or Walls First?

Sounds like the old chicken and egg dilemma. I've heard compelling arguments for both sides. If you do the trim first, you'll spatter paint on the finished trim when you roll the walls. Do the walls first and you have to be extra careful when you cut in the complex trim profiles. The bottom line is that the painting step done last has to be the most precise, so if you are more comfortable painting the walls over to the trim, paint the walls last. I've used both methods successfully, but I prefer painting the walls last, which was the strategy employed by the painting crew in the photos.

roller can lap onto the painted surface and still stay safely away from adjacent surfaces such as the ceiling. I find that the width of my 2½-in. sash brush works well. Work your way out from a corner until you need to reload your brush. Then start a few inches away and work back toward the section you started. This approach minimizes the chances of applying too much paint and creating a drip. Cut in with the edge of your brush, then go back and paint a swath the full width of the brush.

This painting crew used large commercial rollers to paint the main wall areas, but even with standard rollers, there are many areas where a roller cannot be used effectively and that should be painted with a brush during the cutting-in process. Those areas include the spaces between door casings and the ceiling, and narrow vertical areas. Electrical boxes are notorious for holding debris that can stick to a paint roller, so you need to cut in around them as well, including the narrow spaces between a box and the baseboard.

To cut in around tricky areas such as the window-sill and apron profile, use just one end of the bristles to follow the profile. The narrow end of the bristles can be drawn to a point for pinpoint accuracy. Press the point gently into the tiniest areas and then pull the brush away. Fill in all the trouble spots and then smooth over the area with the flat side of the brush.

Before painting the walls, they should be sanded thoroughly. A machine that can be rented makes short work of this stage.

Cutting in walls is generally easier, but there is a lot to be done. To cut in along the ceiling, always start a few inches away and then work back to the completed section.

Areas that cannot be rolled should be painted by hand with a brush, including narrow horizontal sections such as between a door casing and the ceiling (top left), and vertical sections that are too narrow for the roller (above). Cut in around electrical boxes, and paint between the box and the baseboard as well (left).

Get down low to cut in the bottoms of the window aprons so you can keep an eye on the line.

The final areas to cut in are along the baseboard and the corners between wall areas. Follow the same procedure with the baseboard as you did with the other trim areas. Start with the narrow edge of the brush and then go back over with the flat side. Corners are deceiving. There is no finished edge to paint to, so the inclination is to just slop paint on. But it's really easy to apply too much paint and to cause drips, so cut in one side at a time and be mindful of applying a thin, even coat of paint to each side of the corner.

Paint rolling

After cutting in, the rolling process goes surprisingly quick. As mentioned before, the crew here used commercial rollers that were extra-wide, but for most of us nonpros, the standard 9-in.-wide roller pad, frame, and pan are quite adequate. For rolling paint on fresh or primed drywall, I use a roller pad with a fairly short nap, usually ⅜ in. or ½ in. A roller frame (the handle that holds the pad) is an important part of the kit, so just as with brushes, don't opt for the most inexpensive one. Invest in a good frame, keep it clean and in good shape, and it will give you years of service. I also use a telescoping extension handle on the roller frame, which provides better leverage as well as better reach.

Whichever paint holder you decide to work with, dip the roller in so the nap just touches the paint and then roll it back to distribute the paint evenly on the pad. You may have to dip it three or four times before the pad is coated evenly. Avoid dipping too deeply. Otherwise, paint can accumulate on the ends of the roller frame and gum up the axle. When the pad is evenly coated, bring it over to the wall and begin at the

Get down low enough to see the line you are cutting in.

Paint to the baseboard by starting with the tip of your brush and finishing with the full width. Take care not to apply too much paint that can drip down onto the baseboard.

Don't slop paint into the corners just because you don't have to cut in carefully. Paint one side at a time to avoid getting extra paint on the adjacent wall inadvertently.

Paint Pan or Bucket?

If you plan to use a standard-size roller, you can either work out of a 5-gallon bucket with a painting ramp, or out of a paint pan. The bucket holds more paint if you are doing a large room, but it's easier to control the amount of paint on your roller with a pan. If you need to purchase a pan, get the widest one you can for your roller. Narrow pans can be a pain to work out of.

There are two different ways to load a roller for painting. A five-gallon bucket with a painting ramp can hold more paint, but a standard roller pan gives you better control over how much paint you put on the roller (below).

TIP

De-Fuzzing a Roller Pad

One of the most aggravating things about rolling paint is having bits of roller fuzz come off as you roll over the wall. Those tiny hairs create a surface texture that you are probably not trying to achieve. The crew I photographed had a simple remedy. Before mounting the roller on the frame, they wrapped it with painter's tape (masking tape would also work), with the adhesive side of the tape against the roller. When the tape is pulled off, most of the stray hairs end up on the tape instead of on the wall.

Wrap your roller pad in tape, and then pull the tape off to remove all those little hairs that would ordinarily end up in the paint on the wall.

top of one corner. (With a commercial roller, you can work from the floor to the ceiling, but with a standard-size roller, you may want to work about halfway down the wall and paint an area about 3 ft. wide.) Keeping the pad in contact with the wall, roll back up the wall in a shallow diagonal direction. Then come back down the wall in a straight line. Continue this pattern until you notice the pad running out of paint. When that happens, go back over the area you just painted to smooth it out and to even out the coat of paint.

After reloading your roller with paint, start a few inches from the area you just finished and then work back, overlapping the old work slightly to blend the two. From there, work your way across as before, and again, when the pad starts to run out of paint, go back over the whole area to even out the layer of paint. It's okay to overlap the previously painted areas a little, but

if you go over areas where the paint has started to dry, you can "lift" the paint off the wall, which will create an unwanted orange-peel texture and cause spatter on the finished trim. Here are some things to keep in mind as you roll:

- Take advantage of the cutting-in width—don't try to roll too closely to the edges.
- Watch out for the ceiling. It is a pain to clean paint off a ceiling, especially if the ceiling is textured.
- In corners, be mindful of your roller hitting or scraping the adjacent wall. Again, use the whole width of what you cut in.
- Watch out for "ropes," or heavy lines of excess paint, that come off the ends of the pad. If they start to form, roll with just the end of the pad touching the wall to get rid of the extra paint.
- If you are working with multiple cans of a

custom color, blend the cans together beforehand to eliminate any variations between cans.

- When you get into a tight area such as an alcove, shorten the extension handle so you don't bump into the opposite wall.
- For outside corners, always work toward the corner. Avoid rolling away from the corner, which squeezes excess paint from the pad and deposits it on the opposite wall.
- If you notice any flaw in the paint finish from debris on the roller pad, stop immediately and remove it. Then go back over the flawed area to even it out.

When the first coat is dry, repeat the whole process of cutting in and rolling. Just as with the second coat on the trim, cutting in should go more quickly if you've established a perfect line on the first coat. If not, the second cut in is an opportunity to correct those spots. Roll the walls exactly the same as before, creating a smooth and even layer of paint. By the way, if you plan to do the second coat right after the first, you can probably get away with not cleaning your brush between coats. To keep the paint from drying on the brush, you can wrap the brush in plastic wrap temporarily. The same is true with the roller pad.

Start at the top and work down with each fresh roller of paint. Work over in overlapping strokes until the roller becomes dry, and then go back over what you just applied to even out the layer.

5-in-1 Tool Helps Clean Up Mistakes

No matter how experienced or how careful you are, there will be times when paint goes where it's not supposed to go. Always have a clean rag handy and wipe up any "mistakes" immediately before the paint can even think of drying. To clean up hard-to-get-at spots such as the apron return, stretch your rag around the pointed end of the 5-in-1 tool for precision clean up (see the photo below).

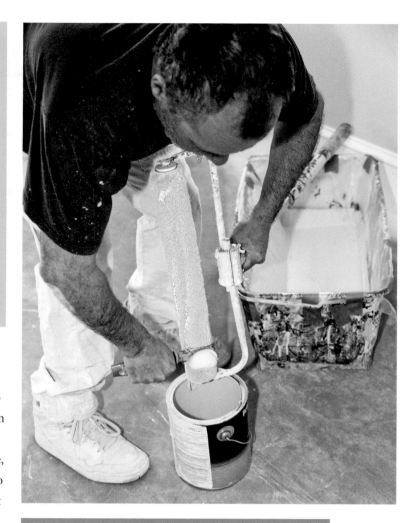

Cleanup

After you finish painting a room, the first priority is to secure the unused paint. Dump any leftover paint from the pan and the cut-in bucket back into the paint can, using your paintbrush to mop up the excess. As before, keep any dried or skinned-over paint from getting into the paint in the can. Your roller pad still has quite a bit of paint in it. Grab that versatile 5-in-1 tool one more time. Use the curved shape and scrape the excess paint into the bucket. Continue working around the roller pad until you no are longer getting any excess paint out of it. At this point, I throw the roller pad away. Cleaning the pad just isn't worth the effort, especially if you've used it to apply a color that could affect a future color that you apply. Remove the pad and slip it into a plastic shopping bag or a newspaper bag so that it can be disposed of without getting paint all over everything. You already know the drill for cleaning the brushes. This time, clean the paint pan thoroughly as well as the bucket, and remember to clean all the excess paint from the roller frame. Stow all your painting tools, and they will be clean and ready the next time you need them.

When you finish painting, use the curved part of a 5-in-1 tool to scrape the excess paint out of the roller.

PUNCHLIST

As you close in on finishing the inside of your house, you will inevitably start to make a list of things you need to finish. As a former contractor, I know that there are always two lists. The first is a list of items that have to be finished before the house receives a Certificate of Occupancy (C.O.)—that all-important legal document that says the house can be lived in—and the second is a list of the personal finishing touches that you *want* to complete or tweak or add to your home.

The C.O. items are most important, so address them first. I purposely avoided discussing the systems—plumbing, electrical, HVAC—because you should always have a licensed professional do those installations. You should have scheduled those contractors to finish their work as you were finishing the carpentry. The plumber needs to hook up all the fixtures that use water and test them. The electrician has to complete all the wiring including the receptacles and switches, installing light fixtures, and hooking up any appliances that require hard wiring. The electrician also puts on the switch and receptacle covers. Just one of those left off could make you flunk the inspection for the C.O. Go through the house with a fine-toothed comb and look for any small thing that might give the inspector pause. Remember, it's always cheaper to have problems corrected while the contractor is there, rather than having to call him to come back.

When you receive your C.O., raise a glass of your celebratory beverage of choice and start thinking about the more cosmetic and less crucial things you want to do to the house. It might be adding that extra shelf in the bathroom linen closet, or putting up hooks and a built-in bench in the mudroom. All these things will happen in good time. And quite often your ideas evolve or inspirations arrive after you've lived in your home for a while. So don't be in a huge rush to finish every last detail right away. It's nice to always have a project for upgrading some part of your home. I'm always reminded of that old do-it-yourselfer's proverb: The person who finishes his house, moves.

INDEX

A

Apron, installing, 121–26
Attic
  access, closet systems and, 191
  air flow and insulation, 23 (*see also* Insulation installation)
  plastic vent channels, 23, 24

B

Back bevels, 123–24, 166, 167, 181, 182
Baseboards, 178–90
  about: overview of, 178
  base cap for, 185–86
  coped corners, 187–90
  estimating materials, 179
  joining, for longer lengths, 184
  pros and cons of installing, 179
  scribing base cap, 185–86
  scribing to floor, 181, 182–83
  starting point, 180–81
  timing installation, 179
  tools for, 179
Basements, insulating, 41–44
Bathrooms
  exhaust fans and ducts, 9, 29, 31–33
  vanity installation, 152–53
Bevel cuts, 118, 122–24, 166, 167

C

Cabinets. *See* Kitchen cabinets; Vanity installation
Casing. *See* Trimming doors; Trimming windows
Caulk(ing), 208–09
Ceilings
  drywalling, 52–54
  insulating, 21, 25–35, 41–44
  trim between cabinets and, 148
Chimneys, insulating around, 32
Closet poles and supports, 190, 193, 196–97, 198, 199–203
Closet shelves, 191–99
  assembling, 195–98
  attaching shelves, 195–96
  attaching vertical supports, 191–93
  cleats and side shelves, 196–98
  measuring and cutting, 194–95
  trimming plywood edges, 198–99
Closet systems, 190–203
  about: overview of, 178, 191
  attic access and, 191
  estimating materials, 191

plans for, 191
poles for. *See* Closet poles and supports
pros and cons of installing, 190
shelves for. *See* Closet shelves
tools for, 190
C.O. (Certificate of Occupancy), 230
Communications wiring, 9–10
Coped corners, 187–90
Countertops, templating for, 149
Cutting
  bevel cuts, 118, 122–24, 166, 167
  closet poles, 203
  door jambs, 101–04
  drywall, 50–51, 52–54, 55–56
  insulation, 24–25, 26, 28, 35–36
  repetitive, fence stop for, 194
  tile flooring, 94–95

D

Dimmer switches, 8
Dishwasher space, 142–44
Doors. *See also* Doors, hanging
  hanging drywall around, 54–55
  measuring for, 99–101
  painting, 209–21
  right-hand vs. left-hand, 100
  switches and, 9
Doors, hanging, 98–111. *See also* Hinges; Trimming doors
  about: overview of, 98–99
  adjusting after, 110–11
  checking level and plumb, 103, 104, 105–08
  cutting jambs, 101–04
  estimating materials, 99
  jamb installation, 101–09
  measuring for, 99–101
  preparing for, 99–101
  pros and cons of, 99
  right doors in right rooms, 99
  setting door height, 101–04
  shimming, nailing jambs, 104–09
  starting with level line, 99–101
  tools for, 99
  types of doors and, 98–99, 111
Drywall, 46–67
  about: overview of, 46–47
  around doors and windows, 54–55
  ceiling, 52–54
  cutting, 50–51
  cutting around boxes/fixtures, 52–54, 55–56
  estimating materials, 48
  finishing. *See* Drywall compound

flat seams, 52
loading into house, 47–49
marking stud locations for, 55
mechanical lift for, 53
moisture-resistant, 48, 56, 60
priming, 67
pros and cons of, 47
screwing in, 52, 53
seams (*see also* Drywall compound)
storing, 49
tapered edges, 52
tools and materials needed, 47
wall, 54–56
Drywall compound, 57–67
  corner bead and, 62–63
  final coat, 65–67
  first coat, 57–63
  flat seams, 59–61, 64–65, 66–67
  inside corners, 61–62, 65–66
  lumps and spills, 57
  mesh tape for, 60
  missed screws and, 59
  mixing, 57
  mudpans and hawks for, 58
  non-square corners, 62
  outside corners, 62–63, 65, 66
  plan of attack, 58
  reinforced tape for, 62
  sanding, 58, 64, 65, 67
  screw coverage, 58–59, 64, 65
  second coat, 64–65
  taping tips, 59–63
  testing for flatness, 67
  tools for, 58

E

Electric
  adding circuits, 6
  checking box labels, 6
  communications wiring, 9–10
  double-checking, 5–10
  drywalling around boxes/fixtures, 52–54
  insulating around, 28–33, 38–39
  lighting, 8–9
  plan example, 5
  receptacles, 5, 6–7
  switched receptacles, 7, 9
  switches and doors, 9
  symbol definitions, 6
Envelope, sealing, 17–19
Exhaust fans and ducts, 9, 11, 29, 31–33

Extension jambs, 117